Breaking the
Cycle of Abuse:

My Journey from Victim to Survivor

Hannah Reinbeck

Published using Amazon Kindle Direct Publishing.

ISBN: 9781983291296
Imprint: Independently published

25% of the proceeds from the sale of this book will be donated to RAINN, the nation's largest anti-sexual violence organization.

RAINN does not endorse or promote this book in any way.

Acknowledgments

To my husband, thank you for all of your support, encouragement and accepting me for who I am. Thank you for loving me unconditionally, embracing my flaws and being so patient with me. You have helped to restore my sense of self-worth. I'm the one who's making out like a bandit.

To my brother, while I was doing my best to protect you and wanting you to have a better childhood; it was you that saved me from losing myself and becoming a complete disaster. Thank you! You have helped me more than you realize.

To Victoria, thank you for allowing me the opportunity to be a part of your journey. It means a great deal to me that when most of our extended family forgot about me, you always remembered. One of my most significant breakthroughs occurred while I was helping you.

To Eleanor, thank you for your compassion, your hospitality and treating me as a member of your family. You were the only role model I had growing up. I look back at that short section of my childhood with fond memories. I felt loved by a family that genuinely cared. I miss you dearly.

To Janis and Seth, thank you both for stepping in and inserting yourself as a means of protecting a child that was not your responsibility. While your actions fell on deaf ears, your effort spoke volumes to me. You are heroes in my book.

Preface

I am a survivor of childhood sexual abuse, and this is my story. The events that you are about to read are true. This story is told from my point of view as I remember them taking place. Anything that took place before I was born or happened while I was too young to remember has been filled in by my mother.

Many of the names have been changed to protect those who are innocent or unaware that these events have unfolded, as well as those who wish to stay anonymous. The name is not as important as how that person chose to react.

I was compelled to get my story out as a means of helping my healing process. There will be multiple breakthroughs, and countless tears as emotional chords are triggered. You're following me on my healing journey as I am experiencing it from my keyboard. It doesn't get any more authentic than that, so get your box of tissues ready.

I've done my best to maintain the events in chronological order as to not jump back and forth in the timeline. You'll notice that much of the content is in a passive voice. Anything written in *Italics is meant to represent my inner monologue or my comments that were only thought at that moment or as I'm writing and reacting to the emotion. Most comments are sarcastic or snarky as that is how I would express myself if I were talking to you directly.*

Sexual abuse of any kind should not be taken lightly. Survivors don't just "Get Over It" and move on. We didn't just have our bicycle stolen which could easily be replaced.

Not only will there be evidence of physical trauma which in time will heal, but very often there will be many unseen emotional wounds that can haunt a survivor for many years. More often than not survivors deal with feelings of guilt, shame, loss of self-worth, sexual inadequacy, embarrassment or have trouble identifying their sexuality. Victims are often made to feel that they "asked for it." I can assure you that no one asks to be violated sexually at any time.

Often survivors are threatened with acts of violence, death threats, blackmail or extortion; which are some reasons why we don't come forward sooner. Most abusers will use that fear, and they know there is a good chance that the victim will not report this crime. I don't care if the abuser has a celebrity status or if they're a big shot district attorney, or if they have covered their tracks and are known to their community as a great humanitarian. Sexual predators are not exclusive to one gender, race, religion or age.

I hope that by sharing my experience, it will help parents talk to their kids and prompt those uncomfortable conversations that need to take place. If you are also a survivor, you may be able to relate and realize that you are not alone. Don't give up. YOU ARE WORTH IT! Maybe you know of a survivor, and you're not sure how to help them; hopefully, my experiences will give you a bit of insight.

It's time that we stop treating this crime as a topic of taboo. The more we can openly talk about sexual abuse, we will raise the awareness of just how often this crime is committed and not reported. There are too many victims still living in silence, and they deserve justice. Victims need to feel safe coming forward without being criticized or accused of only seeking their fifteen minutes of fame. The sooner they come forward, the faster they can start their healing process in whatever manner that is best for them.

Join me in breaking the silence. Staying silent only helps the abuser.

The Survivor Psalm

"I have been victimized. I was in a fight that was not a fair fight. I did not ask for the fight. I lost. There is no shame in losing such fights. I have reached the stage of survivor and am no longer a slave of victim status. I look back with sadness rather than hate. I may never forget, but I need not constantly remember, I <u>was</u> a victim. I <u>am</u> a survivor."-Unknown

Table of Contents

CHAPTER 1:

Putting the Fun in Dysfunction

"Children need at least one person in their life who thinks the sun rises and sets on them, who delights in their existence and loves them unconditionally." - Pamela Leo

I suppose there is no better place to start than at the beginning. Before I get in too deep perhaps a bit of a backstory would help to provide a better perspective when it comes to my dysfunctional family. I would not be here today to share my story about surviving childhood sexual abuse had it not been for them.

No, that is not a compliment, but sadly it's the truth. History of abuse runs strong in my family; in one form or another. I promised myself that this cycle of abuse would stop with me.

My father, Brian was a Marine during the Vietnam War. He was honorably discharged from duty due to a shrapnel injury. He was 30 years old and had been previously married and already had a daughter named Janet. My mother, Marie was in her early 20s, this was her first marriage, and it wasn't long before they had their first child together.

My sister Cassandra was born in September of 1976. She had been born with a severe heart condition. Half of her heart was pumping while the other half did not. From the one picture that I have of her, it is possible that she may have had Down Syndrome as well. Four months later, Cassandra died peacefully in her crib as she slept.

My mother didn't know what to do, or who to call. She was in complete shock, while my father had a temporary mental lapse and could not remember who he was or what was going on. I think it was this moment in time that altered who my father was forever.

Brian's time in Vietnam had come to an end, he was on his 2nd marriage by the age of 30, and he was grieving the loss of his 4-month-old daughter. His way of dealing with things was to turn to the bottle and drink his sorrows away. Marie, while still grieving, she was trying to get back to a sense of normalcy.

Eight months had passed, and Marie became pregnant with me. Brian is still drinking heavily, and he's starting arguments with my mother for the sake of arguing because it was making sense to him in his inebriated state. The top two drunk topics of discussion were: "You better not have another girl, it'll be your fault if I can't have a boy!" Which was followed by "There's no way she's my daughter, you MUST have cheated on me!" *Apparently, my father didn't realize that it was his sperm that determined the gender, not the egg.*

Marie endured nine months of this nonsense and had a very stressful pregnancy. I think a part of her had hoped he'd be a little more accepting once I was born. She had asked his opinion on a name for me, his reply was, "I don't care as long as it's not too hard to spell." I'm less than one day old, and I'm already a disappointment to my father. He didn't recognize the opportunity to make up for what he had lost; he only saw another daughter that won't pass down the family name. *Thanks for keeping an open mind.*

It should not come as a surprise when I tell you that their marriage lasted one more year before Brian's drinking and arguing became too much to handle. It was clear that he was not interested in playing an active or supportive role in either of our lives.

My mother quickly moved on, thanks to her meddling mother Gina setting her up with another military man. I guess back in the late 1970s early 1980s it was socially unacceptable for a mother to be unwed with children. Marie became pregnant again and quickly married Robert. Robert had served in the Navy, and due to his mental state/PTSD, he was discharged. Marie and Robert had their son Joey in the summer of 1980. Robert had quite the short fuse with a volatile temper that followed.

One day my mother was getting ready to pick up a few things at the store. She figured that Robert would be okay watching us for the ten or fifteen minutes. As she's getting ready to leave, she can hear Robert telling us to clean our room. *I should let you know that I'm two-years-old and Joey isn't even six-months-old at this point.* Each time he's asking for us to clean our room his voice gets louder and becomes more hostile.

My mother leaves, and before she can get to the bottom of the stairs from our 2nd-floor apartment, she hears a loud "**THUD**" and her two kids screaming.

Any guesses as to what took place within those 30 seconds?

She rushed back up the flight of stairs to find out that her new husband had thrown me across the room into the wall and he picked up a child's Bugs Bunny slipper, with the hard-plastic head on the toes and threw it at his son, giving Joey a black eye. When she asked why he would do such a thing, he replied, "I had asked them to clean their room, and they didn't listen." *Wait, Wait! I think I have another Father of The Year Trophy somewhere!*

Marie realized she was in a tight spot with her kids and she felt that she couldn't just leave. It must have been like walking on eggshells when he was around, never knowing what might set him off. Marie was hoping for a decent man to help raise her kids, a man that would show interest and look forward to teaching them things and being the father figure that was needed. That is not what she got.

Robert didn't want to have anything to do with me; he felt that I wasn't his responsibility. His exception was to have my last name legally changed before he would consider helping my mother with me financially. So, she went through that legal process when I was three-years-old, but that didn't change the way he treated me.

Robert wasn't overjoyed to adopt me; I still wasn't his. Robert felt that my father should be the one to help take of me, he wasn't wrong. That doesn't excuse his behavior; it wouldn't have killed him to make an effort and show me a little attention and affection or acknowledged that I existed at all. In Robert's eyes, I was damaged goods and not worth the effort or his time. *Perhaps he did have a tiny heart like the Grinch, and it would have killed him.*

Marie and Robert stayed together for another year, and if memory serves they did live separately for the last year as Robert was granted supervised visits with Joey. They did get divorced by 1983 and Robert had moved back to Maine where his family was living. While Robert's family would contact Marie to stay in touch and look forward to her coming up with their grandson Joey, Robert never made an effort to connect with Joey after that. Robert chose a life as a recluse, even from his parents and siblings.

From what my mother has told me, it was my grandmother Gina that had helped to set her up with both Brian and Robert. Marie didn't have a good childhood, her parents Gina and Al were very strict, and their punishments were borderline cruel. Any sensitive subjects weren't discussed because it was too uncomfortable and they seemed to prefer the method of sink or swim when it came to teachable moments.

Some forms of punishment my mom endured included being forced to kneel on gravel rocks sometimes up to an hour. She was hit on her bare backside with a belt as to conceal any sign of physical abuse. There were times after those punishments when she had trouble sitting for a few days after.

She had a hard time understanding how she could get into so much trouble as an only child. She feared her parents, Gina more so and she hated the punishments, yet no matter how good she thought she was, some form of discipline was unavoidable.

Gina was and still is to this day a control freak, always meddling in the lives of her children and never to better their situation but to cause chaos and drama. Marie rarely had the chance to make her own choices; Gina made them. It was a take it and like it situation, even now in her 80's the wrath of Gina continues.

When Marie was 18 she was dating Jon, a young man she met while in high school on her own without the assistance of her mother. Marie and Jon had a great relationship which developed as most healthy partnerships do. Jon was in love with Marie, he did the honorable thing and asked Gina for her blessing to marry Marie.

Gina was not at all pleased and went as far as telling Jon that he better break off the relationship and never contact Marie again. Jon was not expecting that response especially since what he felt for Marie was genuine. Gina threatened Jon. She would go to the police and make a false claim that Jon had raped Marie in hopes that he would take her seriously and that he was never to tell Marie about this conversation. Gina instructed Jon to break off the relationship with Marie and never look back.

I think that Jon realized that he couldn't reason with crazy and he didn't want to take the chance and call her bluff. A false claim like that could ruin his life. Jon did what Gina had asked, and he broke off the relationship with Marie with no real explanation, which naturally came as quite a shock to her since they were talking about marriage.

My best guess is since Gina didn't handpick the one decent guy for Marie, she wasn't about to give her approval. I can understand why my mother had and still has a hard time making choices for herself and always seeks Gina's approval. Gina didn't know at that time just how much of a ripple effect that this break up of genuine love would have. Sure, it didn't affect her directly, only the lives of Marie, Jon, the lives of her future grandchildren as well as the lives of the three kids Jon would go on to have.

My grandmother, the puppet master. Her need to pull strings and cause drama is like a compulsion she can't control, and yet she seems to show no remorse when she turns the lives of others upside down.

Gina was never affectionate with her kids, she would often and still does try to play one sibling against the other as they try to get some form of acknowledgment from her. It's almost like she enjoys teaching lessons the hard way, never teaching in a manner that is nurturing or informative. Gina preferred to throw her kids into the deep end of the pool to see what happens. As a result, her kids aren't working together to get to safety; instead, they are holding each other down to be the first one out of the water.

One example of a lesson learned the hard way is when my mother was in her preteen years; she had noticed a significant amount of blood running down the inside of her legs, she's panicking, has no idea what happened and thinks she's bleeding to death.

Gina avoided having that critical talk with Marie about puberty and what she should expect her body to go through before it happened. Gina decided it was better to wait until the discussion was necessary and didn't see the point in having it before then. My grandmother thinks she's so wise and knows what is best for everyone. She only contributes stress and heartache to those around her.

Are you wondering where my grandfather is in all of this?

From the stories my mother has shared with me, Grandpa Al did take part in the disciplining, and I get a sense that he didn't want to get caught in the cross-hairs of his wife and kept a low profile under the radar. He is in no way innocent, and he too had his idea of "teaching" lessons. Marie was an only child for nine years before my Aunt Cathy came along. Grandpa Al did attempt to "teach" his daughters about sex by exposing his penis to them and molesting them in his twisted attempt at demonstrating how to satisfy a man. Reassuring them that this is how fathers express their love.

Are you wondering if my grandmother knew? From what I gather she did, and she filed that under "Taboo Topics" never to be discussed, just swept under the rug as if it never happened. Seems to be a running theme with this side of my family.

Let's not talk about pressing matters; we know what is best for you even if our actions cause you to drink or you turn out to have self-esteem issues followed by a lifetime of self-doubt. If you're lucky, our efforts will create a mid-life crisis because all of those repressed memories will come flooding back and you'll experience your first mental breakdown. But you can deal with that later. Not to worry, when you come back with questions about the memories you're having, we'll be sure to keep the truth from you even then. It's better if you look crazy than for me to admit I was a horrible parent making those choices on your behalf. I'll never approve of any of your choices. I'm just looking out for your best interest. You're welcome!

That is my interpretation of how it must sound in Grandma Gina's head.

By the time my Aunt Cathy was nine-years-old, Gina and Al had divorced. Grandpa Al would go on to marry three more times while Gina married David and shortly after they had my Uncle David Jr, who coincidentally is only four years older than I am, not at all weird, right?

My brother Joey and I grew up knowing David as our grandfather, and Grandpa Al was just a man that I had heard stories about, and I only recall seeing him a handful of times in my life.

I'm doing my best not to jump around chronologically, but it's essential that I provide an insight into my family dynamic and give you an idea as to the support system I had. Before I continue, allow me to recap the last few pages.

- **My mother, Marie** grew up in a very strict household and endured mental/emotional, physical and sexual abuse by her parents. She was not allowed to make her own choices and continues to struggle with self- esteem and self- doubt daily. The one decent guy, Jon was scared off, and she's been married twice by the age of 25 and has had three kids, having lost her first child very early on. Both husbands were hand-picked by her mother, Gina.

- **My grandmother, Gina** is the puppet master of the family. She meddles in the lives of others. Gina is strict, doesn't show affection, and she never gives without wanting something in return. Gina is the master of sweeping issues under the rug. I'd even go as far out to say that she displays many traits of a narcissist. Gina was married to Al, and together they had Marie, nine years later they had my Aunt Cathy. Gina went on to marry David and together also nine years later; they had my Uncle David Jr.

- **My father, Brian** was in the Marine Corp during Vietnam, he was married once before and had a daughter, my older half-sister, Janet. Brian was nine years older than my mother, and together they had my sister Cassandra, and two years later they had me. The loss of my sister caused Brian to drink heavily, and he became verbally abusive toward Marie. His PTSD, alcoholism, having three daughters instead of three sons was not the life he wanted for himself. Brian eventually moved out of the state and settled in New Hampshire.

- **My stepfather, Robert** served in the Navy, and his marriage to Marie was his first just as his son Joey was his first and only child. Robert's PTSD and temper caused him to be very volatile and physically abuse to Marie, Joey and I. After his divorce from Marie he moved back to Maine and became a recluse and cut off all contact with Marie and barely stayed in touch with his own family.

That brings us to early 1983 when my mother is a single parent with two young children and in my eyes still seeking a suitable father figure for us. Looking back, when one guy left there was another within six months to fill that void in her life. I'm not suggesting she was promiscuous because she wasn't the go out and party type.

I think she was struggling as a working single mother and was hoping to find a man that accepted the three of us and would stick around for more than a couple years. *If I had to bet, it was likely that Gina was putting pressure on her to find another man.*

Sure enough, it wasn't long before my mother was set up on yet another blind date by our neighbor Diane. Diane had introduced my mother to a man named George. I don't know how Diane knew George; it's possible she thought since he was also divorced and a father of two kids that maybe he and Marie had some common ground.

Once George entered our lives it wasn't long before we were uprooted and continuously moving from one place to the next. Mom and George were only together a few months before he convinced my mother to take a very spontaneous trip to Virginia so she could meet his parents.

I was about five or six-years-old at that time, and I recall my mother coming into my room in the middle of the night and telling me we're driving to Virginia, just out of the blue. She was frantically packing enough clothes for herself and us for the next few days, and I still don't know to this day what the rush was all about. It's not like they got married right away. I do however recall meeting Seth, George's son who must have been about nine or ten years old and the five of us piled into George's 2-door Toyota Camry in the middle of the night.

After driving all night some eight to ten hours later and witnessing my first sunrise, we had finally arrived just outside of Richmond, Virginia where the bugs were three times larger, and the thunderstorms somehow seemed much scarier. I remember meeting George's parents and his brother. We spent one night maybe two and drove back to New England. Other than experiencing Dr. Pepper and Mountain Dew for the time, I don't recall anything else on that spontaneous road trip.

It wasn't long after that trip when George moved in with us, and the constant moving around continued for the next three years. As a kid I wasn't consulted, nor did I make it my business to find out why. I was hoping to find a place to settle already.

Due to my mother's upbringing, she made a point to do things differently with us. She allowed us to make our own choices and let us pick out our clothes whether they matched or not and she was honest about the events she had experienced. My mother didn't mind answering questions about our fathers and gave us a chance to make up our mind about whether we wanted to pursue a relationship with them.

One summer evening in 1986 she felt compelled to tell me that she had visited a fortune teller at the local fairgrounds. She was advised and warned about various topics. The fortune teller was concerned about my mothers' inability to learn her life lessons and not receiving another opportunity to fix them. My mother received a warning that the guy she's with now would cause her to lose her kids and she'd never get them back.

Most people might not think much about the unpleasant news and pass it off as "entertainment." I don't know what possessed her to tell me at eight years old, but I was scared. It's not easy to hear your only parent tell you that she could change the outcome, only to pass it off as just a silly fortune teller, then reassure me that everything is fine.

Mom should have listened.

CHAPTER 2:

Empty Promises

"The Difference between promises and memories is that we break promises, while memories break us." – Unknown

When the world is trying to give you a sign, and you ignore it, then a short time passes, and you get another sign, **PAY ATTENTION** and don't discard it.

As much as you might not want to accept the truth or you feel that taking action might hurt your pride in some way; do the right thing and make the necessary change(s). We all have life lessons to learn to help us to grow, to be better versions of ourselves and to help find closure in some fashion or even to help us overcome our fears/phobias.

Don't be so stubborn that you ignore the signs, like my mother. According to that fortune teller, she will not get another chance to better herself in her next life. The choices you make now may have a ripple effect on your loved ones in the future. My life is a perfect example that.

So, not only did my mother get one opportunity to steer the ship in another direction, she received another warning within a few months from an unlikely source. A lady named Janis had stopped by our apartment one afternoon and introduced herself to my mother. Janis was confirming that my mother was in fact in a relationship with George and asked if she had a daughter. My mother was skeptical, at this point; I can't say that I blame her. My mother answered, "Yes I have a daughter" at which point I was asked to go into the other room.

While in the other room I did listen in on what was happening. Janis proceeds to tell my mother it was in her best interest and mine to stop seeing George because he's not a good man. I got the feeling that my mother was uncomfortable but also wanted to know why this stranger is asking these questions and why she'd say such things. Janis was George's wife (soon to be ex-wife), not only did they have a son, Seth but an older daughter as well.

Janis was trying to warn my mother of the sexual abuse that George had put their daughter through in hopes that she could help spare me from meeting that same fate.

My mother was in complete denial, and she was very agitated by this conversation, not upset because my safety was at risk, but angry because she thought it was Janis's way of breaking them up so she could get her husband back.

My mother did confront George and told him everything. George knew how to manipulate the truth and agreed that it was a horrible attempt on Janis's part to get back together. He convinced my mom that any accusations of him sexually abusing his daughter were false and that Janis had convinced their daughter to lie under oath to ensure she would get custody of their kids.

At the young age of 8, this was a wake-up call to me, and it should have been to my mother. I still don't understand how she chose to ignore an obvious sign. A lifeline had been extended from one mother to another in the attempt to ensure the safety of a child she didn't know.

My mother had blinders on, and my best guess is that she finally found a man she felt had accepted the three of us and she wasn't about to let go of that.

After the story of the fortune teller and now this warning appears on our doorstep, literally. I can't help but shake my head and wonder what she was thinking and what her priorities were in that moment.

A few more weeks had passed, and my summer vacation was coming to an end. I recall playing outside with the kids from the 2nd floor. My mother and brother had gone out to run a quick errand. Back then in the mid-1980's the parents in the neighborhood watched out for all of the kids. In my case, the parents of the kids I was playing with were home, and George was around somewhere.

I recall it being very humid this particular day and running up the flights of stairs at the back to get inside of our 3rd-floor apartment to cool off. George had asked where my mom and brother were; I told him they were out running an errand. He asked if I wanted to play a game and I thought it was out of character for him to ask, but why not. While sorting through my toy box, I asked him which one and started listing of the ones we had; Candy Land, Connect Four, Memory, or Old Maid.

*** Trigger warning, continue reading at your discretion or skip to the next page where you'll be prompted by *** to indicate the end of the graphic scene.

None of those seemed to interest him while he leads me away from the toy box and onto my mother's bed. He had another game in mind, a game that started with me on my back while he unfastened my shorts. I knew what he was about to do was wrong and a part of me felt terrible for my mother.

He didn't like looking at me, or maybe it was the idea of me looking back at him; in any case, while he was trying to find something to cover my face I tried to escape before things went any further. I made it as far as the next room before he grabbed me while I'm kicking and grabbing my toy box and anything I can to make it more difficult for him, hoping he'd give up. He didn't.

I was thrown onto the bed, being held down with my mother's black sheer nightgown over my face while he was determined to finish what he had set out to do. As much as I struggled, cried and squirmed I was no match for him. He had both of my wrists pinned down above my head with one hand while restraining my ankles with his legs.

I'll spare you the horrific details and only mention that George was not able to penetrate me on this occasion. The idea of my mom getting home, not knowing how much time he had and the fact that I kept struggling caused him to stop before he wanted to. George made sure to instill some fear in me by warning me that it would be a big mistake to tell anyone about this. George said that he would lie and deny everything, and he knows that he could get my mother to believe him. If I told my mother she wouldn't love me nor would she believe me and I wouldn't be allowed to live with her anymore. Followed by, "You wouldn't want that now, would you?"

George had finally released his grip on my wrists, and he made me promise that I wasn't going to say anything. I put myself together and ran down the back stairs and went behind the garage and cried. Trying to sort out my options and how I was going to handle this. Hoping that would be the only attempt he would make.

*** End of graphic scene.

Just so many thoughts and emotions racing through my mind. *What would my mom think? Would she believe me? While also being so angry with her because she was warned twice about George and didn't listen, so where does that leave me? If telling means I'm taken away from the only parent I know, that doesn't sound like a good option to me,* remember this is my 8-year-old logic.

If I had known that saying YES to playing a game gave him the right to violate me I wouldn't have agreed. I should have said YES when mom asked me to go with her. I should not have gone back upstairs to cool off.

Why didn't I think to kick him where it counts? I feel disgusting, but there is no way I'm going back upstairs alone. What a monster! Maybe I won't have to say anything; perhaps mom will come to realize what a horrible man he is all on her own.

I felt my only option at that time was to keep my mouth shut, keep my distance, do my best not to be left alone with him again and hope that he would slip up and my mother would see what was going on.

The next school season started, and while I managed to keep things together at home, I noticed that my behavior at school was different. Not so much that my grades were being affected, but I no longer wanted to sit with my friends at lunch, and I faked being sick often just to be alone in the nurse's office. I'm not sure why.

Maybe I was afraid of the kids asking questions or them somehow finding out about what happened over my summer vacation. I may have been worried that I would not be able to keep my composure had abuse been suspected. I wish I had a solid answer to that, but I only recall feeling deeply ashamed.

I wish I could say that the rest of this year was uneventful, but it was far from that. It was during this school year that my mother, Joey and I would move a few more times and we would be enrolled in two more schools before the end of the year.

I don't know if mom was having trouble paying the rent or what the issue was or if the landlord wanted us out so more of his family could move in. George had moved out, and he was living a few towns over with his son Seth. By moved out, it was only him moving out and not him breaking up with my mother. *Wishful thinking.*

So, the three of us kept bouncing around from our apartment on the 3rd floor to sharing an apartment with a former neighbor and her son for a few weeks until my mother, and her friend had a falling out. We ended up spending a few nights at my grandparents' house until Grandpa David put his foot down and he kicked us out.

We spent the rest of that night in my mom's 1978 gold Oldsmobile Delta 88 at the end of their street. The police were called, and they came to check out why our car was parked there. The officer saw two kids sleeping in the back seat, they took pity on us and allowed us to spend the night there.

The next morning, we ended up at a motel nearby which lasted one week or two before moving into the shelter and sharing a room with other families with no privacy.

This lifestyle was very stressful, never knowing where I would call home at the end of each school day. Wondering where our next meal was coming from or how long we'd have to stay before being forced to leave.

One thing that did stick out for me during all of that was the fact that my grandparents wouldn't let us stay at their house temporarily until our next apartment was ready to move in.

Allow me to paint a picture for you. My grandparents lived in a four-bedroom house with two full bathrooms, and there was space in the attic and space in the basement, there was a dining room, a living room and only three people living there at the time with only two bedrooms being used.

In fact, this is the same house my mother grew up in, and at that time their house served as a two-family house, one family on each floor. At some point, Grandma Gina and Grandpa Al acquired the entire home for their family.

My grandparents shared the master bedroom, and my Uncle David had the other bedroom. There was plenty of room for another adult and two small kids to stay on a temporary basis while the next apartment became available.

Talk about feeling rejected and getting kicked while you are at your lowest point. It was during this time when I knew I would never be able to count on my grandparents for anything. They didn't want to be bothered or get involved in any way. I couldn't understand what had taken place for them to turn their back on us. This act of selfishness did not sit well with me at all.

It was all well and good that we were expected to show up for Easter, Thanksgiving and Christmas dinners. Our visits were on their terms, never mind the fact that I practically grew up in that house for the first three years of my life when my Aunt Cathy would babysit me so my mom could work.

But then again it was my Aunt Cathy that offered and agreed she would be responsible for looking after me, so my grandparents were off of the hook and could turn a blind eye and pretend I wasn't there.

Come to think of it; they weren't the typical grandparents that got excited when their grandchildren were coming over. We were to be seen and not heard, and we were not to touch anything that was not ours (so basically touch nothing).

We were allowed to only play on the enclosed porch or down in the basement with the toys that were passed down from Aunt Cathy's childhood. My Uncle David rarely made an appearance, and more often than not, I'd catch him sneaking around the house trying to avoid us.

As for my grandparents, Gina would take mom aside so that the adults could talk. Grandpa David would often be busy in his shop across the driveway, or he'd be working in his greenhouse in the backyard. Sunday afternoons, he could be found in the living room watching wrestling. The rule of being seen and not heard was strictly enforced during that time.

I had a tough time sorting out just where I stood with them. Did I offend them in some way? Not likely, as they did not make an effort to get to know me. Maybe they found all kids to be annoying because they were not at all affectionate or eager to impart any wisdom on us. *What was up with Uncle David and why didn't he want to play with us?*

He didn't like to be called "Uncle" David, which I can understand, he is four years older than me, he's still a kid too, so it's a little weird. But it was always said with a negative tone, almost like he didn't want to be associated with his niece and nephew. While we looked forward to playing with him, that feeling was rarely reciprocated.

I had a difficult time understanding why my family was so different and why there was a complete lack of a support system. How could my grandparents be okay with sending their grandchildren to live in a motel, a shelter, or our car?

I knew what my mother has shared that my mom and her stepfather didn't get along. His feelings of dislike were so strong he was not able to set his pride or feelings aside long enough to extend any compassion toward Joey and I. *Was this his way of demonstrating "Tough Love"?*

My mother and her much younger half-brother weren't close either. Mom was 18 or 19 when David Jr came along, and by that time she was already out of the house, so I can understand why there isn't a strong bond between them. It was much later on when more of this story would be revealed. From what I gather, David naturally loves his son David Jr, and he married into our family while Aunt Cathy was about nine years old, and he grew to care for her. Marie was an adult, she had moved out and had kids. David felt he was in no way responsible for her or us. We were not his family, merely a frequent disruption.

To David, the man and only stable father figure type we had growing up, the man we knew as our grandfather felt my mother was an embarrassment, and so were we by association. To him, we were just Marie and her annoying kids, a feeling he shared with Uncle David Jr.

Grandpa David took things a step further when young David Jr asked, "Who's that lady and why does she keep coming over with her kids?" Grandpa David told him "That the lady is a friend of your mother's and those are her two bratty kids looking for a handout." Uncle David wasn't expected to entertain us, nor were we allowed in his room unless he permitted us.

How very hurtful. To feel such shame toward his stepdaughter that Grandpa David disowned her entirely and he lied to his son who grew up not knowing he had an older sister and her two kids were his niece and nephew. No wonder why Uncle David never wanted to play with us, he didn't know we were there to visit with him too.

It just breaks my heart. Even now, some 30 years later to know that Grandpa David felt that way and to go to such great lengths to make sure he didn't get attached or show any interest in us at all when we visited just brings me to tears. Clearly, I cared for him, all while I was nothing more than just a passing thought.

I tried so hard to gain his acceptance, showing interest in his gardening, his hobbies, and I even learned to enjoy watching wrestling with him on Sundays.

Not only have I been rejected by my father, my stepfather and to learn that my grandfather had also turned his back on me. Why am I so hard to love? I wasn't even given a chance. Was it because I'm a girl and they don't know how to relate to me?

David may not have liked my mother, for whatever reason, but Joey and I were innocent bystanders. Would it have killed him to show a bit of kindness or show some compassion? He knew of our situation and knew we were on tough times. Is there some secret Father Code that states a father vows to show ZERO interest in another fathers' kids? It sure seems that way. At this point, I can only speculate as to what David was thinking or feeling.

I guess a better question is, where does my grandmother find these guys and what was it about them that made her think, these guys would make great husbands/fathers? *I'm just pointing out that she is the common denominator with all of them.*

31

Finally, after about a month or two, we were able to move into the next apartment where I finished off my third-grade semester, three schools later. I was happy to be out of the shelter, out of the back seat of my mom's car and in my bed again.

The new neighborhood was on a dead-end street, and there were a few families that had kids our age to play with. Our neighbor downstairs had two boys, both of which ended up in the same homeroom with Joey and I. It appeared as if the sun was finally going to make its way through the storm and life didn't look so gloomy.

I made friends with Amanda and Alison, the girls at the end of the street. The way their duplex was situated there was a good-sized yard to play in at the back with a small wooded area that was great for building forts, exploring, finding snails, little salamanders and helping me to remember that I was still a kid.

While Amanda was a year or two older than I was, we really hit it off and became friends instantly. Just by talking with her I could tell that she had been through a similar trauma. Amanda never came right out and confessed nor was I going to pry if she wasn't ready to share, but she was very knowledgeable about the male and female anatomy and knew more about how those parts fit together better than most 11 or 12-year-old girls do.

Amanda was quirky with a slightly dark sense of humor. She told me that she didn't have many friends, and some kids at school would bully her because they sense that she was different. We shared a similar traumatic experience, and I wasn't going to run away from the "weird" girl. Amanda needed a friend, and I was happy to fill that role.

I'd like to say that my sense of normalcy continued longer than a few weeks, but it didn't. The school year had ended, summer vacation started, and the constant uprooting begins again.

George had been transferred from working security at one Auto Salvage Yard to one closer to his apartment which was now a 20-minute drive from where we had just moved in.

For whatever reason my mother couldn't just spend time with George on the weekends, maybe he worked weekends, or she couldn't find a sitter to watch us overnight, and apparently, my grandparents weren't an option. So, we spent many of our evenings at the salvage yard with George while he was working.

Joey and I had spent most of our summer vacation at the junkyard. We sat around at night while George made his rounds to check the fenced-in perimeter, driving down the rows of mangled old vehicles night after night and spending countless hours in the garage that was poorly insulated and smelled of gasoline and grease. Not at all a place for a 7 and 9-year-old or how we envisioned spending our summer vacation.

It's not like our mother drove us home so we could go to bed at a decent time, no no. If we were tired before she was ready to leave, we slept in the back seat of the car until the wee hours of the morning at which point she'd drive us home, and she'd do it all again the next day.

At some point, my mother had asked him if he would consider allowing us to spend the night at his place.

I suppose all of the late-night driving was taking a toll on her and since he lived in town, she wouldn't have to make the twenty- minute drive back home in the middle of the night, especially if she a had a few beers.

My mother may have also considered that Seth was old enough to watch us and she'd be able to drop us off with Seth rather than make us sit in the junkyard with nothing to do.

Initially, the answer was NO; George and Seth had a roommate who didn't want other people there. Turns out that was a lie. George admitted that to my mother, I never understood why he lied about it. But for whatever reason, he had changed his mind, and we were allowed to visit and spend the night when it was on his terms.

Not only did the uprooting start up again, but so did the sexual abuse.

While we were wasting our childhood in the junkyard, George would send my mom out for food to which of course she was happy to go out and bring back.

He started off safe, making sure Joey went along for the ride and hinting that I should be left behind to keep him company. *Really? He's supposed to be working, performing a job securing the area by rights we weren't supposed to be there distracting him.* But that is how and where the next encounter took place.

The season had changed, the weather was much colder in the evening, and there was a small room maybe 6 feet by 6 feet with a space heater. George saw that I was cold and lured me into the tiny heated room.

George had sent my mom on food runs before so, he had a good idea as to how much time he had. Not only that, but he had to unlock the front gate to let her back in, which also bought him a few extra minutes. These events happened in the late 1980's when cell phones, pagers, and texting didn't exist to the general public. My mother had to honk her horn to alert him that she had returned.

This time George was successful in his attempt, and he would be a few more times. I will spare you the details because once you visually see something, it can no longer be unseen. I will say that there were apparent signs of trauma which I had to absorb with a fast food napkin. I struggled and even tried to reason with him, but again I was no match physically, and you can't reason with crazy. Verbal threats had been made and the fear from six months ago was no longer dormant.

I could hear my mom honking the horn, a sound I was glad to hear. I put myself back together, dried my eyes, took my portion of food and spent the rest of the evening in the car until she was ready to go home. I had to play it off like I was tired as not to raise suspicion since it wasn't unusual at this point that I slept in the car. I made sure to lock myself in, knowing full well that I had the only key. It was all that I could do to protect myself.

From this point going forward; I had started to carry an extra pair of clean underwear with me which proved to be useful.

That time alone gave me a chance to think about my options. How could I alert my mother without telling her directly? She needed to stumble across it on her own because I truly believed that she would not believe me. My brilliant plan was to leave my soiled underwear in a place she would find it, not obvious, but to look like I was trying to hide them (again 9-year-old logic). I had not gone through puberty yet, mom will find them and when she asks if I've started having my periods I could say no, it wasn't a lie. At which point she would be curious and should piece things together. Problem solved, and I didn't have to break any promises.

A few weeks had gone by, she did stumble across my "hidden" underwear and assumed that I had started my periods and thought I was too embarrassed to tell her. *But wait a minute, if she thought I had started, why didn't she offer to talk with me and buy any form of protection or ask if I had any preferences?* So much for what I thought was a genius plan. I needed to be more creative in my approach.

There were a total of 9 encounters within a one-year time frame.

A few encounters took place at the junkyard, each time George would send my mother out for food or beer or cigarettes and in some cases all 3 to ensure he had plenty of time.

Naturally, my mother was sent out for one reason or another as is the case in all of these scenarios. I felt a bit relieved, and confident George wouldn't attempt anything with Joey there. I was sadly mistaken. George felt brave this particular evening and another attempt was made with Joey awake and in the next room.

*** Trigger Warning, continue reading at your discretion. Skip the next paragraph and pick up at the next *** prompt.

Joey and I were hanging out in the small office area; I had gone into the bathroom because I had to go, and George followed me in. He barged in and took me by surprise. I could hear Joey yelling through the door asking if I was okay. I was not okay. I yelled to Joey that "he's hurting me call 9-1-1!" George threatened Joey with bodily harm and threatened to shoot Max (the junkyard dog that Joey had grown very attached to) if he did call for help. George insisted that I had slipped and he was trying to help me. "You don't need to call the police or to tell your mother about this, your sister is fine, and she's just confused as to what happened, she must have hit her head when she fell!" George continues to yell through the door to Joey, "No matter what you hear, DON'T come in here!"

End of graphic scene

Once again, the sound of my mother's car horn in the distance, George goes out to let her in, but not before feeling the need to remind us about Max. A threat we believed because he did have a gun. *A threat that would not have been needed if all I did was slip and hit my head.*

I put myself together and feeling so angry that George had such control over me. I was concerned that he'd turn his aggression out on Joey because he's now a witness. Joey saw that I was crying and asked if he should tell mom. I told him that I would handle it. It was better if he didn't get involved.

I don't know if Joey was aware as to what was taking place or if he knew the extent of the abuse. I certainly wasn't going to burden him with the details. He was only seven years old; there was nothing he could have done that wouldn't result in putting himself or the dog he loved in danger. We never talked about that night since.

Most nights that we spent at the junkyard, I did my best to avoid George. If that meant sitting in our car with the doors locked for several hours by myself, so be it. There was no way I was going to set myself up or make gaining access to me easy for him. I always had "homework" to finish or a "big test" to study for, and I wanted to go to bed early. I would wait until I heard George drive off to make his rounds before I left our car to use the bathroom inside and then I'd rush back before he returned. I had to fake sleeping to ensure that I would not be asked to stay behind on another food run.

It was ironic that there never seemed to be a food run when I locked myself in the car. That tactic held George off, at least temporarily. On a few occasions he sent my mother out to check on me, he was concerned. *How thoughtful of him to "show" any interest in my well-being.*

I also found it strange that my mother never saw my behavior odd enough to question me about it. *Was she completely oblivious or was she afraid of the truth if she had asked?*

If the encounters weren't happening at the junkyard, then they were taking place in his apartment. It's almost like he viewed my attempts at keeping my distance from him as a challenge and needed to reconsider his strategy. At least that's how it felt. I was always having to be creative in making up new excuses.

One excuse I was able to use a few times was that I was spending the night at a friend's house. One of those nights I spent alone in a small camping tent in Amanda's backyard. She recognized that I needed an escape from my home life and offered her camping tent as a place to hide out. While we never confessed anything, it was just an unspoken understanding that we both just knew.

Other times I would make sure I could get back into our apartment by using the window on the back porch before my mother and Joey left. I would go to Amanda's, and she'd keep watch to make sure my mom's car was gone. Then I'd go back and make my way through the window and spent the night safe and sound in my bed. This plan worked great on Friday or Saturday nights.

The other nights in between, not so much. Since the truth about George not having a roommate came out, we were spending many nights at his apartment with his son Seth, who's now 15 years old. Once again, I'm in a position of feeling somewhat safe and thinking there's no way George will try anything with his son and Joey in the next room.

It's not like the insulation was great, the walls were paper thin, and the two-bedroom apartment was small. Each bedroom had a separate door that leads to the bathroom, so there was a good chance Seth, Joey or my mom would walk in. The living room/kitchen was an open concept with no privacy and no way to hide his actions.

As my luck would have it, Seth wasn't always home, and Joey could sleep through anything. Just as every other encounter has started, the ones that happened here also started once my mom was sent out for a food run.

On a side note, just me thinking as I'm writing this out. I wonder if my mother ever stopped to consider why there was never any food in his house or why George's takeout food cravings always happened late night or why he never offered to pick up the food or why he only suggested to leave me behind, not Seth, not Joey just me? Or why did he never packed enough food to last through his entire shift for work?

39

I don't know; I'd like to think that these are things that I would have picked up on. But then again, I'm more open to noticing signs not ignoring them.

*** Trigger Warning, continue reading at your discretion. Skip to the next paragraph to avoid the graphic scene.

On one particular evening I ended up on his bedroom floor by force, I certainly didn't go willingly. No one else is around because, you guessed it, another food run. George managed to convince Seth and Joey to go with her, and he'd stay behind. I was asleep on the couch in the living room.

I was still half asleep when he picked me up from the couch. I thought he was putting me in Seth's room to sleep. No, George placed me on his bedroom floor, and I woke up to him unfastening my pants. I was crying and struggling to get away which only made him upset and more aggressive. He took his gun out from his dresser drawer and set it down next to my head. George told me that if I didn't stop fighting him, he would get a rope and tie me up so I couldn't move. "Stop fighting me; you're just making it worse for yourself, it will all be over soon!"

*** End of graphic scene***

That scare tactic worked, I was terrified. In one breath, George made a promise that this would be the last time, while the next breath he threatened to kill Joey and my mother if I ever said anything. Again, threats I took very seriously, and I was not going to press my luck or put my little brother in danger.

I remember going into Seth's room to lie down on his bed until he got back. It was late, and Joey came in and went right to sleep while Seth came in to find that I had been crying and wanted to know why. I told him that I couldn't tell him so he offered to guess which started off as a few silly thoughts to help cheer me up and without skipping a beat, he knew.

Seth asked how long it had been going on and rather than me sleeping on the floor with Joey that night; he offered to share his bed. Not in a sexual manner, in a big brother protective manner as in my dad will have to go through me before getting to you.

The next morning Seth rearranged his room so that his bed was against the wall, my spot to sleep going forward was between Seth and the wall. Seth confessed that he suspected his father was doing things to me that were inappropriate because his father did the same vile thing to his sister, just as Janis tried to warn us about last year.

I didn't know how far Seth would go to protect me from his father, but there was a small glimmer of hope when I knew Seth was home. Each time I think things are looking up or starting to go my way, I'd get blindsided.

There were a few other attempts made at George's apartment, some successful for him and one where my creativity outsmarted him, and he gave up.

One afternoon when I knew we'd end up sleeping over, I was trying to make it as difficult as possible since there was no way I had a chance physically. I wore two pairs of pants with a belt on the second pair, just in case the first pair on the outside wasn't enough.
Once again, I fell asleep on the couch in the living room, I heard my mom leave and hoped I'd be left alone. Wishful

thinking. George wasted no time turning me from my left side to my back and started working on my pants.

I was awake and fully aware of what was happening, but I was also pretending to be asleep and rolling back to my side to buy some time. George struggled to figure out that the outer pair were button fly jeans and they weren't coming off so easily, thanks to the second pair of pants underneath.

I continued to pretend to be sleeping and moving into awkward positions to slow him down. I could hear the sound of his frustration when he realized what I had done. The second pair of pants had a different fastener, not your typical button or snap, but more of a clasp on the inner waistband that you find on dress pants to hide the fact that there is a fastener.

He must have felt that he was running out of time because he tried to put my outer layer back as not to raise suspicion and I continued to "sleep" until my mother got back. I took that opportunity as my reason for "waking up" and moved into Seth's room.

It was a small victory for me that night. I felt like I had finally found a way to beat him and maybe he'd think twice before putting his dirty filthy hands on me again.

I was expected to keep my promise and keep my mouth shut. I held up my end of the deal. George's promise of it being the "last time" was just an empty promise, an empty promise I heard over and over again.

George had no intention of stopping anytime soon. I suspect the encounters would only stop if he was caught in the act or when my periods started because he did ask and showed interest on that personal matter. *I was too young to make the connection at that time.*

Just as I have mentioned before, anytime I made things more difficult, George increased the risk. Most encounters always started after my mother was sent off for a food run, but this night was different. She was in the apartment making late-night breakfast for her and George.

How do I know this? While I'm in Seth's room, I could hear everything going on in the kitchen, their conversation, the sizzling of the bacon and sausage on the stove. I even heard George tell my mother that he was going to hop in the shower.

Do you recall the layout of the apartment? Both George and Seth's bedroom are attached to the bathroom, and each bedroom had a separate door. While the shower was running and my mom is in the kitchen, I see George coming from the bathroom into Seth's room only wearing a towel around his waist. I assume he came in to borrow socks or a shirt. Proven wrong again, George ups the ante big time.

*** Trigger Warning, continue reading at your discretion. Continue to the next page to avoid the graphic scene.

While Seth and Joey are in this same room sleeping, George goes over to the bed, looking to snatch me out from where he knows I usually sleep and realizes it's Joey. He's now trying to figure out where I am and I'm slowly and quietly trying to make my way further under the cot that Joey typically sleeps on.

Why wasn't I sleeping on the cot? I had learned that I was never safe and this was my attempt at making it harder for

George to gain access to me. Sleeping on the cot was too easy and an obvious place for me to be found.

He searches the cot and realizes I'm not on there. Seth's room was small, George knew I had to be on the floor somewhere. I've been found! He's pulling me out by my legs covering my mouth. I'm grabbing the legs of the cot to slow him down and hope that Seth wakes up or my mom comes in to check on the noise. No one notices, or if they did notice, the disturbance is ignored.

Now I'm on the nasty bathroom floor, struggling while he's covering my mouth in an effort to keep me quiet. He manages to get one leg entirely out of my pants. I'm starting to panic, in an attempt to keep me quiet George's hand is also over my nose and mouth, making it hard to breathe. I ignore his requests to lay still, his promise that this would all be over soon does not make me feel one ounce better.

The sight of my mother walking in does!

*** End of graphic scene***

Oh, Thank God!!! Finally! She has caught him in the act and saw it with her own eyes just how horrible he is. There is no way she can think this is something else, I mean it's pretty cut and dry, right?

She walked in on the scene I had described above and not wanting to jump to conclusions, she asked what was going on, why was I on the floor when he's supposed to be the shower? I couldn't tell if she was confused or concerned as to what she just walked in on.
Before I could get anything out, George tells her that he was in the shower when I walked in from Seth's room to use the

44

bathroom, I was still very sleepy and slipped getting to the toilet.

That answers everything EXCEPT he wasn't wet from the shower, and why one leg is entirely out of my pants. I'm thinking to myself, *Come on mom, you're a girl, you know we don't pee that way.*

For the last time, I put myself together just as Seth walks in from his bedroom to find out what's going on. He's told by George to mind his own business and get back to his room. My mother wants to hear my side of the story in the living room.

Knowing full well George is just going to lie; there is no way I can talk to her under the same roof as him. I grabbed my jacket and whatever belongings I have, ask for the keys to the car, and I told her I would only talk to her out there.

I expect that she's eager to hear my side and should be coming out any minute now. Any minute now….. *What's taking her so long? Hopefully, she's getting Joey ready, and we'll be driving home tonight.*

While I don't know exactly how much time had gone by, I would estimate at least 15 maybe 20 minutes had passed before she came outside to meet me. She asked me what happened and I broke down sobbing and told her everything that that took place. I even apologized to her for not coming forward sooner. I had explained that George had threatened Joey's life, and I had been convinced that she wouldn't believe me or love me if I spoke up.

After she got my version of what happened, she proceeds to tell me what George's version was. He was sticking to the: I walked into the bathroom while he was showering, I was fatigued and slipped while making my way to the toilet story. I had asked her if she thought it was normal for my entire leg out be out of my pants if that were the case. My mother was finding both stories hard to believe.

George wanted her to tell me that he's not upset with me and understood if I was embarrassed. I was welcome to spend the rest of the night in Seth's room.

Again I say, how very thoughtful and considerate of him.

Mom didn't seem too upset, I would have thought she'd be furious and wouldn't want to stay another minute longer. I was feeling a mixed grab bag of emotions. She asked if I was coming back inside. Are you kidding me? *Could she not see the severity of the situation? How dare she ask me to consider going back inside after what I just had confessed?*

I explained that there was no way I was going back inside that apartment, not ever. I wasn't safe. I felt I needed to do something drastic to get her attention, to show her just how serious I was. I told her that I intend to sleep in the car, in the visitor parking lot with the doors locked because it was safer out here than inside with that monster. *My mother didn't appreciate the name calling.*

Even though she thought I was being ridiculous, she left me the keys and said she'd see me in the morning. The front door would be unlocked if I changed my mind or needed to use the bathroom. It was too late to do anything tonight and that we'd get an early start in the morning.

Not at all the response, I had expected. *Was mom really taking George's side even after she walked in and caught him in the act?* She didn't offer to stay with me or come out once to check on me. She went back inside, she talked to George a bit more and slept in his bed until she was ready to leave at 7 am the next morning.

I don't think I slept much that night; I had so much running through my mind. I half expected that my mother would come to her senses and the three of us would drive back home in the middle of the night. I thought for sure she'd break off the relationship with George.

The sun had come up and the next morning had arrived. My mother and Joey had made their way to the car, and I was eager to hear what the plan was. My mother had told me that she had talked with George and did a bit of thinking. Mom had listened to both sides of the story, and the only thing she knew for sure was that one of us was lying but didn't know who. *She can't be serious!!!*

I assured her that I have no reason to lie or make up anything that had happened. She knew that I was an honest kid, even if it got me in trouble. She said that she wanted to believe me. She also wanted to impress upon me that if what I was saying was the truth, it would have serious consequences, not just for George, but for us too and I needed to be aware of that.

I had wondered what more could I possibly go through as a consequence of his actions because whatever it is, I felt that I could handle it. She proceeded to tell me that if I were positive, the next step would be for us to go to the hospital so they could run tests which would confirm who was telling the truth. Tests that would include medical professionals collecting samples with swabs "down there."

If that is what it takes for you to believe me, then let's go! She wanted to make sure I knew what I was getting myself into and was looking for a second confirmation from me before we left the parking lot. I was not super excited about being poked and examined, but I knew I had to do it. Do it for me, do it for her peace of mind, do it for Joey's safety and do it to prove George wrong.

If George knew of my mother's plan to find out the truth, he was probably expecting that I would be too embarrassed or humiliated to go through with it. I'd hate to think about what was in store for me if I had chickened out and George would think that he had won again.

We stopped for a quick breakfast before going to the local hospital. I remember wearing a hospital gown with just my underwear on and socks, being asked to lie down and put my feet in the stirrups so that my knees were close to my chest. Feeling like I was on display was unnerving and emotional.

I wanted to cooperate, but it was hard to relax and remain calm, even now as I'm writing this the tears have started again. I was told what to expect so I would not get startled by the sensation of the swab. I just wanted them to hurry up already. *Couldn't they see I was in distress?* Finally, a sample had been collected, and I was allowed to sit back up and get dressed.

It would take time for the results from the sample that was collected, and the doctor wanted us to remain in that cubicle examination area for just a bit longer. I assumed it was because I was still trying to calm down from my emotional breakdown and they were giving us some privacy.

The doctor came back to discuss matters with my mother, and he also had a few questions for me that were sensitive in nature. The doctor didn't need the results of the swab to know that I had been raped, he was able to see recent trauma to the area, there were signs of dried blood which should not have been there and tearing of tissue that was a clear indicator of forced penetration.

The sample collected was a semen sample and would determine who it belonged to. We didn't have to wait; I knew who it belonged to. My mother brought me in so she could get answers, like them or not, she got them. What she didn't know was that the hospital was obligated to report such cases to the police and child services.

It may have been one thing if this was a one-time event and she brought me right way with the intention of removing me from the situation permanently. I was honest with my answers, and the doctor was concerned that my mother may have known or may have been involved. Judging from my mother's reactions he was not convinced that she was going to stop seeing her boyfriend. The doctor suspected that I was still in danger.

We were met by two detectives that wanted to talk to us separately to figure out what their next plan of action should be. I was not fully aware as to what was happening, but my mother didn't seem too happy, she was scared. I couldn't understand why she found out the truth. I expected she might feel sad, angry or betrayed by George, but I didn't expect her to be scared.

We were asked to follow the detectives to the Department of Child Services for more questions, which again I don't know how much more I could tell them that I didn't already. I remember feeling tired and anxious and just wanted to go home.

I was asked to demonstrate on two dolls what I had experienced, what I was forced to do to him and what was forced upon me. *Not at all humiliating or embarrassing for this 9-year-old little girl. Had I not been through enough already?*

I couldn't help but think that these detectives were intentionally being difficult and possibly hard of hearing. *They heard what the doctor said, they got honest answers from me, I'm exhausted, and now I have to demonstrate a show and tell session, I'm not a toddler that may not comprehend the difference of good touch/bad touch. What more do I have to prove to you? I don't know how else to say it? Is anybody listening to me?! I just want to go home!*

We had spent all afternoon at Child Services. It seemed like no matter how many questions we answered, those asking were never satisfied. I couldn't understand why my mother was being questioned or why it was taking so long. My mother didn't know anything; she wasn't there for any of it, except for last night.

I was more confused as to why grandma Gina had been called in to come down. I figured it was to make sure someone was with Joey who had been spared from all of the questionings. *Poor kid, I can't imagine what's going through his mind.*

How did this whole thing get so big? What was going on? Why aren't my questions being answered? You're the ones keeping us here, why can't you tell me what's going on? When can we leave? Eventually, we were all in the same room waiting to hear what Child Services and the detectives had decided. I'm still not comprehending why we needed their approval to go home. It had been decided that we were going to be assigned a social worker, Sara and she would follow us home. Our mother was to pack a few sets of clothes for us, enough for a few days and Sara would bring us to a foster home to stay for a few days while the detectives come up with a solution.

"Wait, what? Why do we need to leave our home while you make up your mind? Why can't we stay with grandma Gina instead? Isn't that why you called her in here? There is no way mom is okay with this, are you mom?"

It seems mom doesn't have a say in the matter. She was going to comply because she was sure we'd be back home soon, this is just temporary. Her advice was to "think of it as a sleepover." *Now she's giving mixed messages about stranger danger. Why isn't she fighting for us? The one time I hoped that Grandma Gina would stick her nose in, she was speechless.*

The detectives and Child Services just want to make sure our home is safe for you and your brother.

"Safe? Safe from what? Safe from George? Well, that's an easy fix, don't let him come over and I won't go to his work or apartment, simple". *How is it that I am the only one to think of that solution? You're making it more complicated than it has to be.* "Why Joey, he was never hurt like I was? Why can't he stay home, he doesn't understand why he can't stay with you or stay the few days with grandma Gina?" *Can't you see you're scaring him?*

Since mom and grandma Gina were awfully quiet and not going to stick up for us, I had to speak up. I felt their reasoning was unfair and I wanted to be treated as an equal. I can speak for myself, and I wanted to know that Joey was going to be okay, he was innocent in all of this and didn't deserve to be taken away.

I was just so tired of all of the secrets, the private adult conversations about me and no one asking me how I felt about anything.

That was it, the detectives' decision was final. We were allowed to finally go home so that we could pack an overnight bag and Sara would stop by in a couple of hours to pick us up and bring us to our foster home for our temporary stay.

CHAPTER 3:

Is Anybody Listening?

"I like to listen. I have learned a great deal from listening. Most people never listen." - Ernest Hemingway

We had just settled into another apartment that was in the same town as George before our temporary removal. The new school year had started, and we had started our second school within two months.

I remember trying to pay attention to where Sara was taking us, looking for landmarks, gas stations and realizing that we were not close to home. It wasn't a comfortable car ride across the other side of town. Can you imagine being 7 or 9-years-old and being forced to ride with one stranger who is bringing you to live in another stranger's home temporarily?

We had arrived, I was set up to stay with the Thompson family. They were an older couple in their 50's. Mrs. Thompson's sister, Evelyn and their granddaughter, Heidi who was a few years older than me also lived there.

I was nervous, scared, uncomfortable and trying to process the events that led up to this. Then Sara mentions that she has to take Joey to his foster home.

What do you mean, he's not staying here with me? She assured me that Joey was going to be just up the street, only a few minutes away and I could visit him soon. Visit him soon? This is temporary; we were told just for the weekend maybe as long as Monday. "Yes, if everything goes as planned and your mother cooperates you'll be home soon."

After watching Sara drive away with Joey, the only thing I remember is sitting on the floor in the hallway with my bag of clothes crying for what felt like a few hours. I was scared, so tired, doubting if I had made the right decision, feeling bad that Joey managed to get sucked in. I don't know these people; I don't know where Joey is, I don't know how to get back home. What did Sara mean, if mom cooperates? What about school, how am I going to get there or do I have to start over again? So many questions and no one seems to know anything.

The Thompson's seemed friendly, and they let me have my space and allowed me to adjust in my own time. They were getting ready to sit down for dinner, and I had been asked if I was ready to join them. I don't remember having lunch, so dinner sounded good. Their questions for me were basic ice-breaking questions nothing too personal; which was a nice change since the interrogation session at Child Services earlier that day.

Mrs. Thompson reassured me that most kids that get set up at their house don't typically stay very long. If I ended up staying beyond Monday, she would find out where Joey is, and she'd help to arrange a visit for us.

I asked her what she'd prefer to be called; she said that most of the kids that come through called her grandma and that would be okay with her or Mrs. Thompson, it was my choice.

She said that she was asked to take in Joey too, but they don't have room for a boy his age in their three-bedroom house. She usually takes in babies and toddlers for a few weeks up to one month at a time. It had been a while since they had a girl my age and Heidi offered to share her room so that I could stay there. Heidi was excited to have a girl her age to play with finally. So maybe a couple of days there won't be so bad after all.

What had started out as a temporary weekend stay, turned into one full week. That one week turned into two weeks, then we were promised by the end of the month for sure. I had started to lose faith in what I was being told by adults who are supposed to know what is best. Promises are being broken, and nobody could tell me why, just generic answers in hopes that I'd stop asking.

I found that at least Mrs. Thompson was honest and kept her promises on things. I knew there were things she could not disclose and I understood her position, so I never pushed the issue because she was upfront about everything and kept me informed as much as she could. Mrs. Thompson saw that Child Services was stringing me along, not being honest and felt that it wasn't fair of them to treat me that way. She recognized that I had been through a lot. I appreciated that. *Finally, someone else sees what I see.*

The lab results from the swab sample that was taken came back as George's, *no surprise there.* A few months had passed since we had been removed from our home and I was told to testify against him in court and made to relive my trauma all over again in front of strangers. My testimony along with the evidence he left behind sent him to prison. He was sentenced to 10 years with good behavior.

The court system should make an exception for cases like these. Rather than putting a scared child on the stand with all eyes/ears on them, forcing them to relive their worst nightmare over again in that manner should be handled with a bit more discretion.

Why not bring the child into the Judge's Chambers for a private testimony with their lawyers, social worker, therapist or an adult they trust? Their statement could be streamed live into the courtroom unedited or recorded then played back to the jury when the child is not present.

You have no idea just how much pressure you are putting on that child to recall events when their sense of fight/flight kicks in. I certainly wasn't coached as to what I was walking into.

Some children may not perform as well with so many people staring at them. From my experience, I found it very difficult to stay focused because I was busy visually scanning through the crowd to see if George was sitting among them.

Sitting in the stand next to the Judge was intimidating. Being asked to repeat myself because I wasn't speaking loud enough for everyone in the back row to hear me. Feeling frustrated and holding back tears because I thought I wasn't doing a good job. I was having a hard time with the fancy courtroom talk and being too scared or shy to ask them to explain what is being asked.

When are the adults going to think about what this does to the child?

Again, I'll ask, haven't we been through enough? When does the healing begin?

Child Services thought it would be a good idea to arrange for supervised visits with our mother and force us to enter mandatory counseling. Just as I'm settling into my new routine, I'm being uprooted again.

Our sessions were every Thursday which interfered with my last class of the day, just one more thing that didn't sit well with me. It was like putting a spotlight on me with the kids at school always wondering where I was going. Why was I leaving all of the time? Kids don't know how to mind their own business, they keep prying, and it makes it easier for them to single you out.

If they don't get an answer, they speculate, and that is how most rumors get started. I now understand the situation that Amanda was dealing with at school. *As if our home life wasn't bad enough, let's add bullies to the mix just to make it interesting.* As much as those kids think they wanted to know, the truth might haunt them, and they'd be sorry they even asked.

Attending these mandatory therapy sessions was not at all my cup of tea. First of all, it wasn't a private one on one session; it was Joey and me with the therapist.

Nothing at all against Joey, but I didn't want to subject him to all of the horrible things I had endured. Joey was only seven, he didn't know why he had to go, and I imagine that he was very confused. I was forced to grow up fast, and I didn't want that for Joey.

So, after the first "Getting to Know You" session I sat in a chair and pulled the hood from my jacket or sweatshirt over my head in protest that I was not going to speak if Joey was included and made to listen in. *I'd like to think my act of protest worked.* Our one-hour session together was then switched to two individual 30-minute sessions.

Looking back as an adult; these sessions weren't about helping me as it was an attempt to see if my story was consistent and to find out if we were asked by our mother to lie or withhold information.

As for our supervised visits with our mother, those started out as a one-hour visit in a tiny room at Child Services. Our privileges increased over time if we followed the rules and it looked like we were adjusting; meaning we were able to say goodbye to our mother without a tantrum or an emotional breakdown.

The visits upgraded to allowing grandma Gina to join us then to being able to go out in public for a sit-down dinner (supervised) or going to the park for an hour.

A few more months had passed, and there were whispers that we might be going home in time for Christmas.

For the caseworkers who may be reading this, that is something you don't tell a kid if you are not the one making the final call.

While we did not go home permanently, we did have our visitations upgraded so that mom could pick us up to go home for a few hours on Christmas Eve, and then she'd drop us back off. The unsupervised visits were great because they were on the weekends for a few hours. We'd get picked up around noon, spend the afternoon with mom and she'd drop us off by 7 pm.

Those single day weekend visits eventually turned into weekend-long visits that allowed us to spend the night at home. Once again things were looking favorable, and the only privilege we hadn't earned was the ability to go home permanently.

While the overnight visits were excellent, being dropped off was difficult for Joey. Many weekends he'd cry the whole way back, begging our mom not to take him back to his foster home. He promised to behave if she'd let him stay with her, just heartbreaking pleas. He thought it was his behavior that caused him to be taken away.

It was hard for our mother to calm him down and try to explain that it would be just a little bit longer before we could come home. Joey and I had been disappointed by those words before. I understood Joey's frustration, we were doing everything we were told, we've been following the rules. We were so sick and tired of all of these empty promises. *When were they going to stop screwing with our lives and leave us alone?*

Unfortunately, a little birdie had told Child Services that Joey would be very upset and cry after he was dropped off from his visits with our mother. That little birdie was Mrs. Smith, Joey's foster mother.

You put any 7 or 8-year-old in his shoes, and I bet they would react the same way. Child Services keeps dangling a carrot asking us to work a little harder, be patient just a little longer, and you'll get that shiny carrot. When that shiny carrot keeps getting moved farther and farther and the rules keep changing making it impossible to win, of course, he's going to get upset.

I could not understand the logic behind their actions. Joey's just a little boy that wants to be with his mother and cutting back his time to spend with her helps him how exactly? *Ah, to be young and look at the world through kid goggles.*

Child Services thought if the overnight visits were becoming too stressful and upsetting for Joey, then they might have to adjust how often we could see her or go back to supervised visits for an hour. Their choice was to change the overnight weekend visits back to one Saturday or Sunday each month for a couple of hours to see how Joey would respond.

Those whispers of us finally going home resurfaced, there was even a date set within the next month as long as everything was as it should be.

As our luck would have it, everything was not as it should be. You'd think by now that nothing would surprise me. Which makes sense to me now as an adult that I rarely show excitement until I can experience it for myself and see it with my own eyes. I've become a bit of a skeptic in that manner when it comes to good news.

We are on a weekend visit for the afternoon with our mother. Once we get to her apartment (the former home that we spent 2 or 3 weeks in before this mess), she sits us down because she has important news to share. Naturally, Joey and I think, *Finally! Here it comes, when's the big day? When are we coming home?*
Mom didn't look excited; this can't be good news. *Did someone die?*

Seems while Child Services was doing their job, making sure mom was doing everything she was supposed to be doing to get us back home such as:

- Keep her job, to prove she can support the three of us
- Keep a place big enough, so she has room for us when we are allowed back home
- Check in with her probation officer
- Attend her mandatory therapy sessions
- Make sure she gets approval from our foster parents when she's coordinating her visits to make sure someone is home
- Be on time when she's picking up/dropping off and not leaving the state line with us during those visits unless granted permission

- Making sure that she's doing the opposite of what caused her to lose her kids in the first place, no contact with George or anyone else like him.

Our mother had confessed to us that she had been seeing George very secretly, pretty much the entire time.

Our mother had been going to the prison to visit with him and maintain their relationship as if nothing had happened.

What was she thinking? What has she done? How could she do that to us?

The only person Joey and I had thought we could count on had just crushed our hopes. We had thought she was working as hard as we were to ensure we would come home. I don't think I have ever felt so disappointed in my entire life.

What was going to happen to us? Did we mean that little to her? I am beyond upset, I can't stand to even look at her, and I didn't want to hear anything else.

How could she lead us on this whole time, to allow us to get our hopes up just to pull the rug out from underneath us? Feeling heartbroken and disappointed. What is wrong with the adults in my family? Why do our parents leave and never come back? How is it that they can cause so much damage and not see the wake of destruction they leave behind?

Our mother proceeds to tell us that "somehow" Child Services caught wind that she was "seen" leaving the prison. The visitor logs were checked over the last six months, and she had multiple entries. They didn't need to look any deeper; the fact that she had been there at all was a huge No-No.

My mother likes to tell the story that Janis was the one that tipped off Child Services because she's in complete denial and will never admit that she was wrong in continuing her relationship with George. Janis was apparently still very jealous (four years later), and she would stop at nothing to sabotage my mother's relationship with George. Mom's thought process, not mine.

Mom also goes on to tell us that Child Services is forcing her to give up her parental rights. She claims to have done everything they had asked her to do, and yet they are backing her into a corner and giving her the ultimatum of either going to jail or give up her parental rights.

My mother told me that she refused to sign the paperwork that gave up her parental rights, and that Child Services made the choice for her. Our mother had been in front of the Judge numerous times to have our fates decided. Mom said that the Judge was tired of seeing her in there and didn't care what the verdict was. "Give this woman her kids back, I don't care, just get her out of here!" is what the Judge said.

My mother thought she was getting us back. Child Services gave my mother the ultimatum and gave her the papers to sign. Mom brought them home, ripped them up and threw them away. She doesn't see that her choice of staying in contact with George was the deciding factor. In her mind, she never gave up her rights and that's the version that she continues to tell.

The reality is our mother for whatever reason couldn't stay away from George. She thought she was sly, and she got caught. She was hoping to have her cake and eat it too. In her mind she had it all planned out. She'd get her kids back; locks would be installed on the inside of the bathroom door, and on the inside of my bedroom door to ensure George doesn't go in those rooms if I'm in there. She had been brainwashed to believe that George was very sorry for what he has done and he promised never hurt me again.

All should be forgiven, and we can live happily ever after, Right?

I kid you not, that was her genius plan to make sure she could keep her kids and still be with a pedophile. Even, to this day she will never admit any wrongdoing. In her mind, she had justified her actions, and she couldn't understand why she was given the ultimatum. She felt it was so unfair.

Don't even get me started on what's unfair!

Our temporary foster home that started out as a weekend stay turned out to be four years when this moment had taken place.

Meanwhile, our mother is visiting her filthy boyfriend a few times a month and enjoying her parental duty-free life while she's stringing us along, toying with our emotions, giving us false hope, and she doesn't see the flaws in that genius plan.

But she had figured that by the time George would be released, I would be 19, and she thought that I might be moved out by that time. That still doesn't make me feel any better about being under the same roof with him. *What if I didn't move out at that point? The bathroom and my bedroom would not be the only two rooms he'd consider committing more vile attempts against me. Does she even hear what's she's saying?*

I don't think it occurred to her that if her genius plan worked, pedophiles don't change, they lie. Time served in prison is not even close to a cure, nor are they rehabilitated because they "found" religion. So don't be fooled and buy into that garbage. Those that commit sexual abuse are only sorry that they got caught. In many cases abusers are often abused by their one of their parents, this is true in George's case. He was sexually abused by his mother when he was a young boy.

If that ridiculous scenario became a possibility, you could bet your ass I would not have stayed knowing he was being released and expected to have a place to stay with us. How dare she even think that was a perfectly fine and acceptable solution?

Mom thought it was best that we heard that news from her before Child Services told us and they would most likely suspend our visitations. She was trying to give us a chance to ask her questions before we didn't have a means of making contact. *I guess I can't fault her for that logic.*

Sure, we had questions, lots of questions behind the waterfall of tears in our eyes.

The most prominent question being, "What's going to happen to us now?"

She had suggested that we were most likely going to stay in our respective foster homes a little longer while Child Services would try to find a family that would like to adopt both of us.

Just when I think the news couldn't get any worse.

It's hard not to make the comparison that you are no different than a dog in a pound, discarded by its first family because they lost interest and now you're waiting for another family to hopefully come along and see how special you are if given a chance.

I had zero interest in being adopted; I wanted no part of it. In my mind (now 13-years-old) I was quite content with the Thompson's and felt confident that I would be welcome to stay under their care. I was so tired of moving and starting over. I was finally in a happy home where I felt that I belonged and where I was safe. Joey seemed to share that feeling about his foster family. He had grown to see Mrs. Smith as his mother figure, and he had friends in the neighborhood as well as a particular dog in the house that he loved.

Uprooting yet again didn't seem like it was really in our best interest. We were happy, why mess with that?

Can't we consider Grandma Gina and Grandpa David or how about Aunt Cathy and Uncle Jim, can't we live with them?

According to our mother, Grandpa David said "NO," and Aunt Cathy wanted to help, but their place was not big enough. There would have been room for me with my two younger female cousins, but Joey by rights should have a room of his own, and they could not afford a larger place to accommodate both of us. They felt it was unfair to take me in if they couldn't take Joey too.

Our mother made it very clear that if she "couldn't" keep us then she wanted us to stay together. I use that term "couldn't" loosely, she could have but chose not to keep us

CHAPTER 4:

House of Chaos

"People will forget what you said, People will forget what you did, But people will never forget how you made them feel." - Maya Angelou

Once the new phase of adoption arrived, so did our new caseworker, Martha. I was not a big fan of Martha; I don't know what it was.

Maybe it was my misplaced frustration that I may have directed at her as being the bad guy helping us through the adoption process. Perhaps she was so darn chipper that I found her happiness to be annoying because my life was so miserable. Maybe it was because she had entered my life when I had lost all faith and trust when it came to the adults deciding what was best for me. I was waiting for the other shoe to drop, expecting she too would disappoint me in some way.

Then again, maybe I didn't realize how my emotions had altered my perception of this lady who was only trying to do her job.

Martha if you are reading this, I'm sorry for giving you such a hard time…. You've just witnessed a breakthrough, folks!

At this point, my mandatory counseling sessions still going on and my therapist thought it was in my best interest to start going to group therapy with other girls my age working through the same trauma. I wasn't a fan of the one on one sessions, but I went every week which I'm pretty sure had decreased down to once a month at this point.

I was not a fan of having to talk and relive the same moments over again. I just wanted to move on already. I was well aware as to what happened; I was there. But, I went anyway because I didn't have a choice in the matter. Much like most things that were done in my best interest.

This new group consisted of one counselor/mediator, one adult volunteer/sexual abuse victim and four other girls in their early teens. I could tell from their body language that the other girls were just as excited to be there as I was.

I'm feeling better because I'm not the only one that doesn't want to be here. We had been asked if any of us were there by choice, NOPE. Which was a good ice-breaker, we all chuckled realizing that we also had that in common and we may as well make the best of it.

Over time I grew not to despise group therapy altogether. It was nice to know these girls could relate and I didn't feel like I was the only one. It was easier for me to open up and share things because it felt safe, unlike my private sessions where I felt like my responses were being examined under a microscope or being twisted in some manner. I hated phrases like: "So, when you say, blah blah blah, what you're really saying is bloo bloo bloo." No, when I say, "blah blah blah, I mean blah blah blah."

Group therapy was an eye opener in the sense that just when you think you have it tough, there is always someone that has it worse. I was secretly jealous of those girls that were home with their family and didn't have to experience being taken away.

On the other hand, those are the same girls that turned to alcohol, drugs/pills, became sexually overactive or experimented with self-mutilation to cope, or had thoughts of suicide as a possible solution. I felt lucky to have not considered any of those options.

The topic of adoption was a subject I had tried to ignore and avoid. In my mind, this idea was just a horrible solution, and there wasn't anything anyone could say to make me think this was really in my best interest.

The way I saw it, considering our mother had given up her parental rights, she no longer should have a say as to what happens with us.

Why after four years of living apart from Joey was it so crucial that NOW we stay together. We were only a two-minute drive away from each other. We could call each other anytime, and we rode the same bus on the way to and from school for a few years. In most cases, we were invited over to each other's birthday parties. Again my 13-year-old logic.

I had been in the foster system long enough to see dozens of kids come and go. Some kids stay a few nights, a few weeks or maybe a month until a family member steps up and takes responsibility. I knew that babies and toddlers were quick to find new families because it was an easier adjustment or transition for both parties involved.

Older kids like Joey and I take much longer to find a family. We have memories of our family, friends and our previous life. Most couples want to have the full experience as opposed to five to seven years before those kids move out and move on.

Not to say that it doesn't happen, it does. I lived with two sisters at the Thompson's while their older brother was placed in another home. After two and a half years all three of them were adopted by the same family when they were five, nine and eleven years old. So it does happen, but the process is much longer, and the transition isn't always as easy when you're dealing with preteen and teenagers.

I was waiting for Mrs. Thompson to speak up and offer that I stay there. To let them know that I was well adjusted and part of the family and they were happy to remain my legal guardians.

I was never consulted on this matter, as had been the case thus far. *I was only 13, what could I possibly know at that age?* I had learned to become a silent observer, having witnessed more than I should, listening when most thought I wasn't paying attention and knowing more than I let on, learning to read body language and facial expressions.

That is what I learned while being excluded from conversations about me and my best interest. I've also developed a keen sense that detects liars and hidden motives which is also handy.

I don't know where you're from, but what I had in mind for this whole adoption process, it wasn't like any adoption scene I saw in any movie. What I had envisioned was an agency or a section with Child Services that was dedicated to adoptions and matching families with a child(ren) that was best suited for their lifestyle, done in a private setting.

For example, Mr. & Mrs. Kelley walk in, they are interested in adopting a little boy between newborn and 24 months old and would prefer if the child had Irish or Scottish roots. The agent would confirm if such a child is available and the process would continue until the Kelley's found a match.

Maybe I watched too much television or my overactive imagination was in high gear… But hopefully, you see where I'm going with that thought.

Martha picked us up and drove us to an adoption event that was being held outside at a park one summer afternoon. There were at least one hundred kids with their caseworkers from all over the state with just as many potential families looking to adopt.

I remember having to wear a name tag so that a potential family could approach and try to get to know me. Also providing them a chance to see if I was going to be a good fit for them. For me, I found the whole process to be utterly humiliating.

I felt like I was on display being auctioned off. I could almost hear an auctioneer calling out; Here we have a 13-year-old teenage girl with brown eyes and blonde hair, she's in her last year of junior high school, isn't she cute folks! Young Hannah is pretty responsible for being only thirteen. She gets herself up and ready for school, she's well-mannered, and Hannah aspires to become an artist. This is a GREAT DEAL folks! Not only will you be bidding on Hannah, but her younger brother Joey too! Joey's full of spunk and energy, he'll keep you on your toes! Young Joey loves animals and aspires to become a Veterinarian. Let's say we start the bidding at $100, $100 to the couple at the picnic table. Do I hear $200, $200 going once, $200 going twice, SOLD to the lovely young couple by the maple tree. Congratulations folks, you've bypassed the diaper changing, late-night feeding stage. These two will be out of your house in no time!

Joey and I had been at this event for a few hours, and during that entire time, I had TWO families stop and talk with me. Joey is off running around and playing with the other kids, so at least one of us is having a good time.

The first family asked my age at which point their response was a disappointing, "Oh! You look younger than 13, sorry we don't want a girl already in her teens." They wished me good luck and walked away.

Do you have any idea how much that hurt? This is something I haven't thought about in over 25 years, and yet it still hurts just as bad as it did when I first heard it. What a crappy thing to say to a kid.

While I'm sure at that time they didn't mean to offend, but for the love of god, remember where you are and who you're talking to. Instead, it was a reminder of just how disposable I was. Rejected again without being given a chance.

The next family showed genuine interest in us. They lived over 2 hours away across the state and owned a large piece of land with a few farm animals. They tried to sweeten the deal by mentioning they had a couple of ATVs that we could use to get around the property and wondered if we liked outdoor activities.

Joey liked the sound of that. Meanwhile, all I could think was they only wanted older kids for free labor to help with their farm animals. I was not at all wanting to move across the state to an unfamiliar area. I was secretly hoping this wasn't going to be our only offer.

Turns out that it was not our only offer. While the couple at the adoption event was interested, I think that trying to coordinate a time to get to know us would prove to be very difficult with a 4 to 5 hour round trip included. That family ended up backing out.

A few months had passed and finding a new home for us was proving to be difficult. Joey's foster mother, Mrs. Smith, realized the situation we were in. She had previous experience adopting older kids and took pity on us. Mrs.

Smith offered to take me in to ensure that we could spend the rest of our childhood together.

Martha had stopped by to tell me the news in person and relaying how happy my brother is and wanting to know what I thought about it and if this arrangement would be okay with me.

I was not overjoyed as I weighed the pros and cons:

PROS:
- Joey is there, and it would help with my transition while I move again.
- I know this area, and I wouldn't have to change schools or reapply to another vocational high school.

CONS:
- I've been to his foster home a few times, enough to know that at least ten people were living there with only one bathroom. Never mind all of the animals.
- There is a total lack of privacy because there is so much commotion and so much noise.
- I didn't want to share my room with a bunch of toddlers; I would never get any peace living there.
- CHAOS, SO MUCH CHAOS

I felt like an ungrateful jerk telling Martha that I don't see why I have to move at all. I appreciate Mrs. Smith's offer and thinking about us, but I don't know why I can't stay here with the Thompson's. I didn't want to be adopted, nor was I okay with having to change my last name at this stage of my life.

Martha's response was something along the lines of, "We at Child Services feel that you've been in foster care long enough and there isn't a reason why you shouldn't be adopted at this point and settle into a more permanent home." In their eyes, foster homes were meant as a temporary placement until a permanent home could be established. Then she laid on the guilt trip; if I was to continue staying here at the Thompson's, then I was taking away one spot for another little girl that needed it.

Well, thanks for making me think that I actually had a choice in this matter! I should have known better. You ask for my thoughts, and they are discarded because it's not what you want to hear. You were hoping for a big smile and a happy dance, but instead, I rained on your parade. Not because I'm ungrateful or enjoy being difficult. I know what I want and where I would be happiest. I'm speaking, the words are coming out, but no one is listening!

I don't think I even had one month to mentally prepare myself for what would be the next phase in my life. Things just seemed to happen very quickly. The day of the adoption hearing was upon us. In attendance: me, Joey, Mrs. Thompson, Mrs. Smith, Martha and the judge.

The judge had recapped the situation to make sure she was clear about who was going where and who was adopting who. Joey and I had been asked if we understood what was happening and if this is what we wanted to happen. Now would be the time to speak up.

I made it known that I was aware as to what was going on and that I was NOT okay with it. When asked which part, I said that I didn't want to be adopted, I didn't want to have to change my last name. At which point Joey spoke up and also said that he didn't want to change his last name either.

When asked why I didn't want to be adopted, I said that I didn't see the point. I was going to be 18 in five years, and I didn't understand why I couldn't just stay with the Thompson's until then. What I got in return was, right now my only option was Mrs. Smith who was kind enough to offer to take me in so I could be with Joey. Unless I wanted to take my chances and get set up with a family that I didn't know and go without Joey.

I was assured that I didn't have to change my last name, rather than adoption, the only other alternative was for Mrs. Smith to agree to sign on as my legal guardian and relinquish her responsibilities when I turn 18.

What other option did I have? Clearly, I didn't have any other choice.

There were forms to fill out, and signatures were required in various spots. Just like that, I went from a ward of the state to property of Mrs. Smith.

It wasn't until the car ride home with Mrs. Thompson when she said that if she had been given the option to become my legal guardian, she would have gladly agreed. It seems Child Services never thought to ask her how she felt. The only thing Child Service kept pressing the issue on was that Joey and I were to stay together.

Child Services never expected that The Thompson's would be interested in becoming my legal guardians. They knew that they could depend on Mrs. Thompson if they ever needed to find a safe home for a baby or toddler in a last-minute situation. I was never expected to stay as long as I did as far as Child Services was concerned.

That was a sad day for both of us. It's a sad moment even now.

The day has come where I'm expected to move out of the happiest home I've ever known during my childhood and start over yet again. A home that I know isn't the right fit for me. It makes me sad to leave; I'm angry and frustrated because my words keep falling on deaf ears.

Mr. Thompson helped me pack my belongings in the car, and he drove me up the road to Mrs. Smith's house. I was a little disappointed that Mrs. Thompson didn't come to see me off, but I knew she would have a hard time, just as I am having a hard time now.

I don't recall having much to take with me, and I know that I left a lot behind. I wasn't sure how much room I would have, and I thought it was better to bring the essential items because I was confident that I would be welcome to go back to retrieve more of my things later on.

I was welcomed by everyone, not in a happy you're here sort of way, but due to so many people in one house you were always crossing paths with someone. They were all accustomed to having new kids come through, and my arrival was no different.

Mrs. Smith said that the master bedroom upstairs was mine. There was a kid's bed in there meant for her younger adopted daughter, but she never sleeps in it. Some of the drawer space was free for my clothes, and she cleared some space in the closet. I was warned that she'd have to come in from time to time because her desk was in there, and that is where she took care of her bills. There was a crawl space off of the closet, so I should expect that someone would have to go in there from time to time to get access to the attic/storage.

Once again, allow me to paint a picture for you.

Originally this house was a four bedroom with 1.5 bathrooms. The layout at the time when I moved in consisted of:

- Two bedrooms and One full bathroom on the main level, as it was originally.
- One Master bedroom upstairs, which was original
- One small 6' x 6' bedroom upstairs that used to be the half bathroom
- A second bedroom upstairs, as it was originally
- One 8'x 8' bedroom in the basement with access to the meter
- A two-room suite consisting of a small bedroom and a small living room

At one point there were up to 14 people living in that house:
- Mrs. Smith
- Her retired stepfather, Pete and her elderly mother, Gram had the room off of the kitchen
- Her 18-year-old son, Jesse had the tiny upstairs room
- Her 22-year old daughter, Leah with her husband, Dominic and newborn daughter in the two-room suite
- Her 24-year-old daughter, Cindy adopted as a child in the other basement room
- Her 24-year-old son, Todd adopted as a child who was treated as the live-in babysitter shared a room with Joey
- Her youngest adopted daughter, Natalie 9-years-old, shared a room with Mrs. Smith
- Two young foster kids, sisters, 3 and 5-years-old, also shared a room with Mrs. Smith

- Joey was 11 and yours truly, 13-years-old

Never mind the four dogs, three cats, rabbit, guinea pig and bat. Yes, with wings.

I threw myself into my school work as my means of escaping what had become my new reality. I tried to keep myself busy and dreaded walking back into that house.

Some of you may feel that I may not have given this new environment a chance; maybe, I should have been grateful that things worked out in the manner that it did.

I attribute these five and a half years that I spent here as the pivotal time in my life when I, Hannah the pistol, Hannah the firecracker, Hannah that tells it like it is and doesn't take any shit, no longer existed.

It was at this moment that I, Hannah the quiet, soft-spoken, Hannah the doormat that was always being taken advantage of, Hannah the all too eager to please others and would often sacrifice her happiness, Hannah that no longer had a voice to speak up for herself had emerged.

Sometimes I amaze myself; we have another breakthrough! That only took twenty-seven years, better late than never.

As an introverted person, I had never had an issue spending time by myself. I'm not a complete hermit; I do enjoy getting out from time to time to experience new things and traveling. The time I spend alone or in the quiet company of others is my time to recharge, my time to think and reflect.

Living in this house of chaos was a constant drain on my energy, a continuous drain that never had the chance to recover fully. I'd get home from school, and before entering the house the first thing would hear was the sound of kids screaming, adults yelling, and one tiny overprotective dog snarling and attempting to bite my ankle.

There was always so much yelling, not because people were upset or fighting with each other (although it happened regularly), but you felt like you had to talk over each other to be heard. It was exhausting. All day, every day.

So, it's no wonder why I came home and went straight to my room and hid in there; especially on the weekends. Weekends were worse because everyone is home. The little kids would wake up early, and there was never a chance of sleeping in past 7:00 am. Most weekends I woke up to the songs of Barney & Friends playing over and over and over while listening to the high-pitched screams of the little kids fighting over something petty.

Where was an adult to step in and supervise these kids? There were six adults over the age of 22 living there. Had they learned to sleep through it? It didn't take long to see how this family dynamic worked. Most of the adults took the stand that it was Mrs. Smith that kept bringing these kids into the house, she should be the one taking care of them. It's almost like the roles had been reversed; these little kids were turning on the TV, VCR and they'd let themselves outside to play. When the kids asked an adult for something, the response was to "Go ask Ma." *Could the other adults not decide what was right or wrong?*

It turns out the adults were in the habit of not getting involved; these kids were not their problem. I was living in a house full of tattletales and busybodies who just had to know everything, not because they were genuinely interested but only so they could say, "I'm telling Ma!" I can't even count how many times a day I heard, "I'M TELLING MA!"

Every weekend it was the same all over again. It felt like the movie "Groundhog Day." The little kids would wake up and set themselves up to watch Barney & Friends for the 200th time. They'd walk into the bedrooms of the adults one by one for help, and each one would yell at them to go away, go upstairs, you'll have to wait until Ma gets up. The little kids would get tired of waiting and either Natalie or I would get them cereal or toast and give them juice in a sippy cup.

I would stay downstairs with them until Mrs. Smith or another adult offered to take over. There was no way I could ignore the fact that two little kids were being left unattended. Typically, an hour or two had passed before any adult would surface. In many cases, someone would make an appearance long enough to see that the kids were being watched and then they'd return to their room.

Once in a while I was told that I didn't have to stay downstairs and watch them, that so & so was awake and could listen out for the little ones. *If so and so had been awake this whole time, why didn't they come out from their room? If they were awake and knew I was watching them, why didn't they come forward?*

I suspect they were enjoying their peace and quiet and didn't want to be bothered. They were relieved no to get involved. *So happy I could take one for the team while the rest of you are caught up in your self-absorbed bubble.*

Just a bunch of lazy good for nothing mooches. That alone was my motivation to do well in high school, graduate, learn a trade, get a job and move out as soon as possible. I didn't want to become the next live-in full-time babysitter with no prospects.

Mrs. Smith worked as a bus driver during the school season. Her stepfather, Pete would sign his social security check over and only keep enough for gas, tobacco for his pipe and some spending cash. The other adults were not contributing for their use of the utilities or food, although sometimes they bought their own, but most times they didn't. So how was Mrs. Smith able to pay for everything?

In a heated conversation, it had slipped that Mrs. Smith was getting a check every month from Child Services for each kid she took in. Money that was meant to help feed, buy clothes for that child and purchase school supplies or diapers. That money was not intended to support the seven adults and eight pets residing in that house. That explains it, the more kids, the more money coming in.

While Mrs. Smith may have started out taking kids in for the right reason back in the early 1980's, but she's not taking them in for that reason anymore. Both her biological adult kids and her two adopted adult kids were still living there rent-free, as far as I knew. From how it appeared they weren't in a rush to move out any time soon. Why should they, they had a pretty sweet deal going at the house of chaos?

This environment was not at all conducive to helping children cope with their trauma. It was a madhouse with daily verbal arguments, and sometimes it got physical between Jesse and Dominic. I witnessed an act of animal cruelty as Dominic kicked one of the dogs down a flight of stairs because it pooped on something that belonged to him. Dominic had kicked this dog so hard that this 30-pound dog had lifted from the floor high enough to break a lamp on an end table.

Joey was distraught, that was his dog that kept getting abused and blamed. The physical altercations sometimes when beyond Jesse and Dominic and they would team up against Joey. It had not been the first time these two had put their hands-on Joey. They didn't see a problem with physically assaulting a boy half of their age.

What did Mrs. Smith do? Nothing! Joey shouldn't have provoked them to lose their temper. That was how Mrs. Smith handled those situations. *How very nurturing and protective of her.*

Even Mrs. Smith's mother, Gram was a piece of work. Natalie was her favorite; Gram groomed that little girl to be the biggest tattletale of them all. Natalie was the eyes and ears of the house and had no problem getting in your business.

Gram was cruel with her words with the foster kids and with Todd. She would often talk down to the kids and say things about their parents and how unfit they must be for the kids to end up in this house. Todd didn't have it easy either, he was insulted on a daily basis and treated like garbage.

Due to the abuse and neglect that Todd endured as a toddler by his biological mother, his neurobiological development was stunted. While Todd was an adult, mentally he was much younger. Jesse, Dominic, Leah, Cindy and Gram constantly reminded Todd of that and often told him that he wouldn't amount to anything. Todd had been groomed to be the live-in babysitter, the caretaker of all of the pets, the housekeeper, the groundskeeper and Gram's in-home assistant.

Joey often heard "Just because your last name isn't Smith doesn't mean you don't have to listen!" and "Just because your last name isn't Smith doesn't give you the right to talk back"! Most everything that came out of Gram's mouth was vile.

A foster home is supposed to be a safe place for kids; this one was quite possibly worse than some of the homes these kids are forced to leave. I honestly don't know how Mrs. Smith managed to stay on as a foster parent for as long as she did.

I focused my attention on my school work which kept me busy along with getting my first job at sixteen at the local country club. A few of my friends also worked there which made it helpful to carpool if Mrs. Smith was too busy to drive me. I certainly couldn't count on the other adults to offer me a ride to work.

My choice to go against the grain and enroll in the vocational high school was not popular with my friends that wanted me to follow them to the public high school.

I realized that the only person I could count on was me. I had to do what was best for me. I didn't have parents to help me. I didn't have an adult that encouraged me. It was in my best interest to develop a useful trade to help find work, or at the very least to have a marketable skill to fall back on.

Most of the programs had a high probability of being male dominant. It was common for most girls to enter the Allied Health program. I was drawn to the Automotive program.

There had yet to be one girl to enroll and successfully graduate from the Automotive program. Challenge Accepted!

I was determined to see this challenge to the end and prove to myself that I could do it. I also wanted to show other girls that it was okay not do what is expected just because that is what 95% of the girls have done before them. I also felt it was vital for me to know the basics when it came to vehicle maintenance and knowing how to change a flat tire or to boost a battery.

The instructors were great; they often went above and beyond to help the students learn and understand the material. I expected to get dirty looks and be the last one picked when we had to pair up with a partner. While most of the boys didn't have an opinion, there was one who made it very clear how he felt. I was the butt of his jokes, the target for his insults and in his closed mind; I had no business being there. I knew that this wasn't going to be easy. It certainly was not easy, for one second.

This cruel boy was a thorn in my side for the entire four years. He teased me relentlessly and made sure I felt incompetent and useless in hopes that his efforts would cause me to quit. I had no intention of letting him win or get the best of me.

In the 85-year history of that vocational high school, I was the first female to graduate from their automotive program. Upon completion of this four-year program, I had received two "Excellence in English" awards and was recognized for my "Outstanding Citizenship." All of my hard work had paid off, and my efforts had not gone unnoticed.
Thanks to my automotive instructors, they had set me up with a part-time job at one of the local Chrysler Jeep

dealerships. I started out filing the repair orders by make and Vehicle Identification Number for the Service Department after school. On the weekends I worked in the office as a receptionist answering the phone and paging over the intercom.

I was 17 and had recently graduated. I loved working here; my coworkers quickly became my second family. I was more impressed that they held a little graduation celebration for me with a big cake, balloons, a card signed by everyone and an offer to work full time.

During my time working here; some of my co-workers would turn into lifelong friends. It was from this connection in which I was able to finance a vehicle that came with a new driver insurance policy that wasn't cheap.

I'll fast forward a bit to the event that caused me to leave the house of chaos.

Cindy had confronted me about how I should be paying rent if I wanted to stay there or I should think about moving out. I was not expecting this conversation from her; as we rarely spoke over the last five years, and it caught me off guard.

She goes on to tell me she can see that; clearly, I'm making money, I have a newer vehicle and that it was time I stop hoarding my money and start pitching in. *I don't understand where this is coming from or why she felt that it was her business.* I had explained to Cindy that I had only been working full time for a few months at this point, and with the vehicle payments and insurance I didn't have enough saved to move out yet, but that was my plan. If Mrs. Smith thinks I should pay rent, then I'm happy to have that discussion with her. I didn't see where it was any of her business.

Cindy felt the need to remind me that I eat the food. To which I replied, that it had been weeks since I've had a meal in this house. She goes on to remind me that I do use the shower and electricity and that I wash my clothes there which cost money. I took my clothes to the laundromat because the one washer/dryer was always in use by the thirteen other people with mounds of clothes waiting to go in next. I didn't appreciate her butting her nose in where it didn't belong.

When she was done giving me a piece of her mind I went upstairs to see if Joey knew what that was all about, maybe he had heard something. Mrs. Smith preferred to communicate with me indirectly. She'd tell Joey or in some cases complain to Joey about me.

I'd have to hear about whatever it was from him which was often followed up with, "Did your brother tell you"? I don't know why she didn't feel as if she couldn't approach me herself. She had no trouble confronting anyone else in that house directly. Everyone else seemed to know her issue with me before I did. I was always the last person to know.

Joey had not heard anything and thought it was in poor taste that I was confronted at all by someone in their late 20's and still renting a room in the basement. He passed it off as jealousy because I was doing better (at 18- years-old) than the other grown adults in the house (they were always borrowing money). Maybe they were jealous that I had plans on moving out while they had become complacent.

I was not aware that I was competing, I was doing the best that I could to set myself up to finally move out. I needed a good job, a reliable vehicle and enough for first month's rent and a deposit, which I was working toward. Joey suggested that I should talk to Mrs. Smith when she gets home to confirm if that is what she wants. I did just that.

When Mrs. Smith came home, I let her know that when she has a moment I wanted to run something by her. It was often hard to get her attention when she first gets home because she's often bombarded with the kids and her mother wanting to tattle about something petty.

When she had a moment, she caught my attention. I proceeded to tell her how Cindy confronted me about paying rent and what her thoughts were about it. I was confused as to why I had to hear such things from somebody other than herself.

She sounded annoyed and had suggested that Yes, the issue of me paying rent is a little overdue. I had been allowed to stay (2 months) beyond my 18th birthday, and she had assumed I would have started paying rent by now. Frankly, she was surprised that I had not come to her to work out an arrangement. "It costs money to live here, and your **free ride** is over!"

I was again, taken by surprise and now profoundly hurt. How was I expected to know to start paying rent if I'm not approached to have that conversation? We had never talked about it, not once. I was asked to go through my expenses and get back to her with an amount that I felt I could contribute every month.

It was now my choice if I wanted to continue living there or find another living arrangement. That didn't sound like a choice to me. I don't have enough money to move out yet. It was expressed that my lack of funds wasn't her problem.

That conversation did not sit well with me, not one bit. It wasn't the idea of paying rent that bothered me. I have never had a problem paying my way or contributing my share. *Free ride? What free ride?*

It was the childish manner that she went about it. If you are going to treat me as an adult, then talk to me as an adult. Don't send in your enforcer to do your dirty work and make it seem like I chose to avoid paying rent over the last two months.

Had she been referring to the last five years? Was she holding her choice of taking me in against me? Had my presence in that household been such a financial burden? Did her choice of adopting Joey and becoming my legal guardian cause her to lose state-funded income? I was trying to be financially independent, so I was less of a burden, how did that backfire? I had been doing my laundry since I was 13 and when I was able to drive myself, and I paid to have it cleaned. Was I oblivious as to what was expected of me? Had I just been kicked out?

I let Joey know what the outcome was and that I wasn't sure what I was going to do. He didn't want me to leave, but I didn't want to stay, I felt defeated. Knowing what I know now and how Mrs. Smith felt, how could I live there? I went to my room and made a few phone calls to see if there was any chance that I could stay with a friend or if there was an extra room that I could rent.

That's right; I had been paying for my land line since I was 16 because I was tired of Natalie not giving me my messages or just unplugging the phone from the wall while it was in use because she wanted to use the phone. With so many people, there were always calls coming in for someone else. Trying to use the main landline for more than five minutes was very difficult.

89

I had been let down and strung along again. I had been just a number this whole time. The offer to take me in wasn't for my benefit; it was for her own selfish needs. It was clear that I was not wanted there. If I wasn't wanted, I wasn't going to pitch in a single cent.

Within a few days, I had an opportunity to move out. During those few days, I was repeatedly asked what I had decided. Not that it was their business, but I let the inquiring minds know that I was leaving. I needed a few days to pack and sort out the details. I was treated horribly and asked why not leave now if I had somewhere better to go. Dirty looks from the bullies were received as if I had betrayed them somehow. They were forcing me out, and I wasn't leaving fast enough for them.

I was set to leave later that week; instead, I ended up going that night after work. The process was very rushed and very emotional. I thought everything was fine and somehow the grown adults had turned against me, no warning shot was fired, just a full-blown ambush.

Joey was upset with how Cindy, Gram, and Mrs. Smith handled this situation. He took it upon himself to confront Cindy which in his mind started this whole thing. She initiated this and continued to harass me until I left.

I appreciate his effort in his attempt to stick up for his big sister. Cindy was less appreciative of Joey's concerns, and her solution was to start a physical altercation with him. Joey was sixteen-years-old at the time, while Cindy was almost thirty-years-old and should have known better.

What the hell is wrong with the adults in this house? Just because these kids are not your kids and their parents aren't there, doesn't give you the right to put your hands on them or abuse them in any way.

I continued to pack what I felt was most important, things like tax information, important papers that I couldn't replace, whatever clothes that would fit in any small suitcase, a set of bed linens and my pillow. My room was a mess from the frantic packing that had been done very last minute. I was too upset to attempt to organize it; I just wanted to leave as quickly as I could and never look back.

Joey helped me pack my belongings in my truck. I remember carrying my things through the kitchen to get to the back door and nobody offering to help. Nobody said goodbye or wished me well. Just glares and words muttered under their breath.

Joey walked me to my truck; we hugged, said our goodbyes, shed a few tears and I apologized for leaving him there alone. He understood why I couldn't stay. I wasn't able to hold the tears back once I drove away. I felt horrible. I felt torn between wanting to stick around for Joey and not wanting to continue to be a punching bag and bullied for trying to better my situation.

I called Joey after I was settled to let him know I was alright. He had informed me that after I had left that night, the adult residents felt his wrath. Verbal abuse coming from the adults seemed perfectly acceptable, but it was not acceptable if your last name wasn't Smith. As for the belongings I left behind, Mrs. Smith was not pleased with the mess I left behind. The vultures didn't hesitate to pick out what they wanted before throwing the rest away.

Maybe I was impulsive with my decision, but I was fired up. I was forced into an impossible situation. I was just an outsider whose time had run out.

Please tell me again that moving here was in my best interest!

CHAPTER 5:

Hurricane Max

"You will never understand the damage you did to someone until that same thing is done to you. That's why I'm here." — Karma

I was happy to be away from the house of chaos. I didn't realize that most of my wardrobe consisted of mostly black and white pieces until it was brought to my attention. I didn't own anything in any other color; my work uniforms were the exception.

I didn't go through a goth or emo phase nor did I ever resort to the use of drugs, alcohol, smoking or partake in any other harmful habits. Though drugs, alcohol, and cigarettes would have been accessible in the house of chaos; I never inquired. Wearing dark clothing was my subconscious way of showing how I was feeling on the inside.

I had made a promise to myself when I was 8-years-old that I would never get involved or experiment with drugs or start any addictive habits. I can proudly say that I have kept that promise 32 years later.

Being forced to leave the house of chaos; I had been offered to stay with my boyfriend (at that time) and his father. They had family in Florida and were in the process of making plans to move back. When I mentioned having to "sort out the details" earlier, this is what was pending.

I was now responsible for myself; I didn't have to run my choices by anyone. I gladly accepted the offer to move down to Florida with them. They were confident that I would help pay for my share of things and that I'd find work to continue pitching in. I did just that. I was grateful to have been given a chance.

It just so happened that they required a means of transportation to drive down. I had such a vehicle that I was happy to offer. I needed a place to live, and they had a spot waiting. Funny how things work out sometimes.

The three of us strategically loaded the bed of my truck as best as we could, and we piled into the front cab. We drove 18 hours straight before stopping in Georgia to sleep for the night.

I had spent the next two years in Florida with a great family. As much as I truly appreciated their hospitality and taking a chance on someone they didn't know, my romantic relationship had come to an end. Once again, I packed my little truck and made the long journey back home to start over again.

You'll start to see that I have become quite the nomad, never staying anywhere for too long. What started out as a curse has become a blessing.

I had rekindled a former relationship with my former boyfriend from Junior high school. Max and I had an on again off again puppy love that began when we were 13 and 14-years old. So young, yes, I know. But we had a great friendship, and Max's family recognized that I was having a hard time at Mrs. Smith's house. I had spent so much time with Max and his family, that they considered me family from the first day I was introduced to them.

Max and I celebrated our birthdays together since we were only one year and one day apart. I also spent many holidays with them and used to babysit for Max's youngest sister. Even though it had been a few years since I last saw Max, we always kept in touch. We had an uncanny telepathic connection and could sense when the other needed to talk with a friend. We were that listening ear or a shoulder to cry on for each other.

When I returned home from Florida, I was welcomed to stay with Max and his family. I remember getting in late that night and arriving when everyone, except Max, was sleeping. He let me in, and I made myself comfortable on their couch. Max's father came out, noticed me there and gave me a little kiss on the top of my head and whispered, "It's good to have you back; Max has been miserable since you left."

I had no idea writing that would cause me to be so emotional, that was almost 20 years ago.

Max and I were officially together and engaged. I was given his grandmother's engagement ring to wear. Max's father, Jack was happy to pass the ring down, and he was proud that I was the one wearing it.

Eventually, Max and I moved out; in fact, we had moved two more times before finally getting a place to ourselves. I found work at the local Auto Parts store where I would spend the next five years before being offered a position back with my dealership family. I was happy to accept that position and work with everyone again.

Max had found full-time work picking orders and delivering auto parts for a small local distributor. Max had never been on his own; he had always lived with his parents. So, this idea of having to be an adult and budget money to pay bills, rent, utilities was very new for him.

He was finding that his new full-time job was getting in the way of his band practices. At this time, he was juggling two bands that required his presence at each band practice; which was sometimes twice a week with a live show on the weekend.

Max was a self-taught drummer and a darn good one. If he wasn't playing his kit; he was constantly air drumming with sound effects to go along with it. Air drumming the table, the dashboard, and steering wheel while driving. His hands and feet were always going.

Over the next few years I had attended countless band practices and somehow took on the role of Max's drum technician. Helping him load the kit, set it up, tear it down, and reload them back into my truck. It was fun at first, being able to tag along and watch him play, but somehow my presence at his band practices and his live shows had become mandatory.

That is how I spent most of my weekends over the course of four years. Trying to decline was an invitation for a guilt trip. I couldn't understand why I couldn't just stay home and relax while enjoying an evening to myself. It would have been a nice change from the constant noise, feedback from the amps, the screaming into a microphone, and the banging of the drums.

It's not like I was a member of the band, I was merely a silent spectator. It was exhausting. I didn't see the point of going to all of the band practices if I was expected to be at the live show. It was hard to show any enthusiasm for music you've heard live 100 times; music that was not my preference. Screaming hardcore music and mosh pits just wasn't my scene.

I just thought I was being supportive and showing an interest in Max's passion. I didn't realize what this behavior was going to lead too. The signs were there, and my coworkers expressed concern for my well-being. Since I

didn't have any experience to pull from, I didn't recognize the warning signs and defended his behavior.
Oh God, I sound like my mother.

Max and I were married during our fourth year together; I was twenty-four and Max was twenty-five. We had lived in a one-bedroom apartment within a multi-unit apartment complex in which Max's oldest sister, Shelly had also lived with her wife, Tess.

Max's employer had made arrangements for Max to attend a conference in Georgia. The meeting would span over three days to cover the new products that one of the brake manufacturers had developed. The company was paying for the round-trip train ride as well as the hotel for the nights he was staying over, and there was a bit of money for meal allowances.

Max was not at all excited about this trip; in fact, he was dreading it. I didn't fully understand what his hesitation was about. It sounded like a great opportunity; I think there was a part of me that was happy to get a bit of a break. I was excited about the idea of doing nothing while he was gone.

Because Max and I worked in the same industry, we saw each other often, and many of our customers knew who we were. I was working in the Parts Department while Max would make weekly deliveries to my place of work, so my co-workers also knew who he was.

Over the next year, my co-workers noticed a change in my attitude toward Max. I went from happy and smiling to annoyed when his name was mentioned, and they saw that I had lost weight to an almost unhealthy level at the low end of the spectrum for my short/petite frame. I had become irritated by the constant calls from Max while I was at work.

At first, it was sweet that he was thinking of me and wanted to coordinate our lunch breaks. It didn't take long before these phone calls escalated to calls about nothing of importance. Max was bored, and he would go through the four people he talked to most. His mother, Linda or his best friend, Lou or Max's sister Shelly, or it was me.
Max would talk to his mother several times a day, and he'd call while she was at work. Max would do the same with Lou, and if Lou was too busy, he'd call me. I kid you not, this happened every single day.

His constant phone calls were getting me in trouble with my boss, and it had got to a point when we saw his place of work show on the caller ID, my boss or co-worker would ask if they could help him, I was unavailable even when I was standing right there.

It had come to a point where my workplace was my escape from him until he started making deliveries every week. I desperately needed space; I had been smothered for too long. Always doing what Max wanted to do, going to band practice until midnight only to get up at 6:30 am the next morning for work, his constant phone calls felt like borderline harassment. Why couldn't he respect my need for space or accept that I needed time for myself?

Thanks to the invention of cell phones, Max had another resource of getting in touch with me. The idea of a cell phone was great as I intended to use it for emergencies. I did find the cell phone handy at work while I was out delivering parts. Otherwise, I didn't have any friends that I talked too. The only phone numbers I had programmed were my work, home, and Max's cell phone. Max's friends were my friends by association. I didn't expect anybody to call me because the only person that did was Max.

I have always been a creature of habit once I have a set routine. Max would know my work schedule and knew to expect me home by a specific time, give or take a few minutes. Max had a hard time accepting that some work days would run a bit longer than other days. Some customers needed more attention than others. Some days I was out on a last-minute parts delivery that ran longer than expected. Max would call my work, and if I weren't there, he'd try my cell phone (which I quickly learned to put on vibrate).

God forbid my day ran a bit longer than usual, it was worse if he called and I ignored him. I got an ear full about how concerned he was that he couldn't reach me. I needed to keep the volume on my phone up so I could hear him calling (that didn't happen). I wasn't trying to stress him out. Enough was enough! If I wasn't home and I wasn't at work, then I was on my way to one or the other. That was my life, HOME, WORK, BAND PRACTICE. That was it.

I dreaded being called at work when there was nothing to say. I was busy at work with customers and technicians relying on me to do my job. It's great that he had some free time in his day, I wasn't so lucky.

He couldn't understand why I sounded annoyed when he'd call. Suddenly, I was the bad guy. *Shame on me for being annoyed when you're calling only to say HI for the fifth time today.*

The day of Max's trip for work had arrived. His overnight bag was packed, and I was trying to keep his spirits up during the drive to the train station. The train ride would take a good portion of one day each way the plus the conference would last three days. I was excited to get five Max free days.

I'm sure some of you might think I'm horrible for thinking this about my husband. I swear I'm not as cold-hearted as my inner monologue makes me out to be. These events are real; they did happen. I own every feeling and thought that I share within these pages.

The only plans that I had, while Max was away was to carry on about my usual mundane responsibilities. Get up, go to work, come home from work. Maybe I'd stop and pick myself up something for dinner or perhaps I'd stop to visit Joey to see how he's doing. I wasn't planning a raging party or going out to the bar, that was not my style.

Max called when he arrived at the hotel, a call I was expecting for peace of mind sake. I received another call the next morning before his conference started, just as I'm trying to leave for work. I get home from work, and I'd have a message waiting for me on the answering machine. The message doesn't seem out of the ordinary, just summarizing the events of Max's day and that he'll try again later to get a hold of me.

I decided to go out and visit with Joey for a bit before he started his overnight shift. I was there maybe an hour before heading back home which was a five-minute drive. I had a few messages on the machine, all of them from Max. Each message he left; I could tell by his voice that he is worried, and there is a sense of panic that grows deeper with each message.

First Message: He's asking if I'm home, you should be home by now, he's worried.

Second Message: Same as the first with more panic and worry in his voice.

Third Message: He's scared, I don't know where you are, I've called your work, and you're not there! What's wrong? Why aren't you home yet? Why aren't you picking up the phone? I'm calling my mother to have her stop by after her shift from work to check on you!

Fourth Message: I'm calling Shelly and having her stop by, and make sure you're home! Why aren't answering the phone? Where are you? Please, please, please call me back when you get this!

Fifth Message: Max is in full-blown panic mode, He sounds terrified and has imagined the worst thing possible. Why isn't anyone calling him back! He's coming home early!

Max left five messages in one hour and ten minutes while I was visiting Joey. I had just finished listening to the last message when Shelly and Tess knock on the door. Shelly knew Max was overreacting and tried to calm him down; reassuring him that she's sure that I was okay. If I had decided to step out after work, she was confident that I wouldn't be gone long. Shelly was doing her due diligence to appease her brother.

Max did get a hold of me. He called as I was talking with Shelly. He had worked himself up so much that he was trying to convince his boss to arrange for him to come home early.

He didn't believe everything was fine at home. We are unable to convince him to stop worrying; there was nothing unusual going on. He had one conference day left before leaving the next morning to come home. Even his boss could not convince him to stay in Georgia as planned; it was just one more day. Max got his wish; his boss had arranged for him to leave the next morning.

He was not handling his time away from home alone very well. As previously mentioned, Max had never been by himself or away from home for any length of time in his twenty-seven years. There was always someone with him; whether it was his family, friends, neighbors or a member of his band.

It was all making sense. A few years ago, Max had gone on tour across the northern USA, and up into Canada with his band and another band from New Hampshire. They were gone for about two weeks, and Max didn't have any problem being away from home or sleeping in unfamiliar places during that time.

How had his insecurity gone unnoticed for so long? Max had a fear of being alone; which explains why when he's just sitting around he would call everybody until he finds someone who's not too busy to talk with him. But why was he so smothering?

I had realized that he had always frowned upon me spending any time with anybody other than himself or his family. If I wanted to go out or spend time with anyone, he was coming with me, or I'd get a guilt trip and give in to his selfishness. I didn't have friends that were mine; I wasn't allowed to hang out with my co-workers after our shift. During this time, I was not on speaking terms with my mother or grandma Gina (that's a story for later).

My social circle consisted of Max, his family, his bandmates to which I am still just a silent spectator and his best friend, Lou which included Lou's wife, Tina and their young daughter, Lexi. I had the honor of being Lexi's godmother. (also, another story for later).

This lifestyle had gone on for almost four years until we bought a computer and I was introduced to AOL, various online games and a particular MMORPG (massively multiplayer online role-playing game). I was intrigued, a little behind the times as a Xennial, but still interested to finally experience the online world. There was a chance for me to have a social life, the ability for me to interact with other people outside of my bubble, the bubble that Max created for me.

Eventually, Max and I moved out of our one-bedroom apartment and bought our first house. Max's boss's mother was selling this house. I remember going to the open house and falling in love with it instantly.

The house was a two story older colonial with a screened in front porch and a small fenced in backyard. As you walked in from the front porch, you entered into a blue shag carpeted front room. To the left through a set of french doors was the hardwood floor living room. Through the front room, to the left, there was a large full bathroom with an older style claw foot tub.

Beyond the bathroom was a huge kitchen; which was great for Max, he enjoyed cooking. At the rear of the kitchen was a mudroom that leads to the backyard. To the left of the kitchen, there was another carpeted room with a large walk-in pantry. On the left side of that room, there was a door that leads into the bathroom with the claw foot tub.

Upstairs there was a bedroom on each side of the staircase. Farther back was a makeshift kitchenette with a sink, stove and a small closet area for storage. Behind each bedroom, was an access area to the attic space and another small storage area.

There was more room than the two of us needed, but we had talked about starting a family. This house was big enough for us to grow into, should that happen. The location allowed for us to be closer to work, so that was also a nice feature.

We were both excited to become homeowners.

The only downside to having a home that has an extra room or two that are not being occupied is that your house becomes an Inn for family and friends who suddenly need a place to stay. That has been my experience anyway.

That is what happened after two months of just getting settled and feeling like it was our home. Max's sister Shelly had a falling out with Tess, and she needed a place to stay while their house was being sold. We took in Shelly, and within a few weeks, Shelly's new girlfriend and her two young boys were also staying with us.

That arrangement lasted a few months before they moved into the apartment next door. It wasn't long after Shelly left when Max's father Jack needed a place to stay.

Max's parents were always arguing, for as long as I have known them, they had rarely agreed on anything. But this was different. Max's mother Linda was done arguing over the same things time and time again. Three of their four kids were out of the house, and she felt that it was time for Jack to find a place of his own.

Linda had not been happy in years; she had stayed in that marriage as long as she had because both of their incomes were needed to keep their family of five going.

I was finding it very difficult living in my own house. It was becoming less of mine and more of Max's family's home. Still no peace and quiet and no time for me to relax.

Jack had been laid off, so he's home most of the day eating our food and not replacing it. Since we let Shelly take the two twin beds that were in the spare room, Jack was occupying the pull-out couch in the living room with the french doors. That is where he spent most of his day, watching TV and eating with little motivation to find another job or look for a place of his own to live.

By some slim chance that Jack wasn't around and I think we have the place to ourselves for a bit, Max would take that opportunity to play his drums in the basement. The sound just echoed throughout the house. Max was not a part of any band at this time, but he was happy to have a place to play whenever he wanted.

I was finding it difficult to be so accommodating to everybody all of the time and keep up the facade that I'm perfectly okay with everything. I was so tired of living with other people. People that would come and go at all hours and lacked a sense of being courteous. Max's brother would come over to spend the night without asking; it was just assumed Max was okay with it; therefore, I would be okay with it.

I was not okay, not at all okay! I felt it was a complete violation of my privacy and my personal space. Max's family and their friends coming over unannounced using our home as their local hang out while we weren't home. Not cool! I could tell that Max was starting to get annoyed, but he wasn't going to put his foot down with Jack. Max did tell his brother to stop bringing his friends over. That didn't last, as his brother would bring them by while we weren't home because Jack would allow it despite our wishes.

I didn't have a safe place, not at work, not at home, no friends, no family (mostly). Once again, my concerns are falling on deaf ears. My husband can't/won't control his family as they are taking over our house. There is a complete lack of respect for our belongings, our privacy, and our home had turned into another house of chaos.

Since our TV was always in use, I spent more time on my computer playing online games and learning my way around an MMORPG that had become popular with some of my co-workers. This was my attempt at feeling like I was part of something that didn't include Max. I needed something that just for me.

I was able to pass the time by playing various games, earning badges, and chatting with other people from time to time. It was a nice change, a change that didn't go over very well with Max.

Max would often hover over my shoulder while I was playing and chatting. He felt the need to warn me that I should be careful with talking with people online. Some very disturbed people might try to get private information from me. He was afraid I might lead someone to our home, and they'd kill us. *Thanks for your confidence in me.*

While I appreciate his concern, I wasn't having those kinds of conversations with anyone I was playing a game with online. I wasn't looking for a booty call; I was making small talk, and in most cases, we were helping each other earn badges. Nothing more. Max never saw it that way and insisted that he wanted to read through my chat history to verify that I had not compromised our top-secret location or that a guy wasn't trying to seduce me.

Max's efforts didn't stop there, and now he had a whole new reason to be paranoid (so he thought). I realized that he had been going through my emails and search history when he brought up something mentioned in an email; a topic I had not discussed with him. I wasn't hiding anything, but he sure made it out that way. He was treating me like a deviant, lying, cheating spouse. In some cases, he was treating me like a child.

I'd try to talk to him and explain that he's taking things out of context. He only saw my attempts and reasoning as a means of deception. In his mind, I was lying and trying to cover my tracks. He would confront me about innocent things all of the time. My responses were never good enough or acceptable. Max was so sure I was hiding something, and he was determined to discover the truth. The truth was, there was nothing to find; it was all in his head.

I've said it before, and I'll say it again; You can't reason with crazy. Maybe I should rephrase that. I can't reason with crazy.

This madness continued over the next the 11 months. Max's family would continue to live with us, and our home was their hang out. My time on the internet was closely monitored and blown out of proportion.

Our marriage was suffering, and the act of sex which was tolerable had now become an obligation. I declined many of Max's advances, which only upset him. I had been accused of cheating because if I wasn't having sex with him, I must be getting it from someone. Max had suspected I was cheating with a co-worker. *I'd like to know when I had time for an affair; Max kept a close watch on my whereabouts. Second of all, GROSS!!!*

He felt that I was the one responsible for making him worry and feeding into his fear of losing me. Max made it clear that I needed professional help and he was going to make an appointment for me. I didn't have a say in the matter, I was going to talk to a therapist of his choice, and he was going to ensure that I went and made an effort to fix our marriage.

Wow! Talk about being blindsided again. I was aware of my issues when it came to my hesitation in the bedroom, and he was fully informed as to why. Max was the one person I thought would understand because as a young teenager he was molested by a friend of the family during his early teenage years. His encounter made him second guess his sexuality while we were dating years ago. *Hence the on again, off again phase.*

Max's sex drive seemed to suddenly increase, mine was not so willing to keep up. I found it very difficult to get in the mood with other people in the house. It was unnerving to feel that at any moment someone might barge in because his family had lacked a sense of privacy. Sex was rarely the first thing on my mind; I had yet to find it enjoyable. My experience had proven sex to be self-serving for the other person.

Which makes sense as to why I react the way that I do now. I apologize if some of you find this to be a little TMI (Too Much Information). But I can't help when the breakthroughs happen or what triggers them. It is for that reason why I'm sharing my experience with all of you.

Max made an appointment with his former high school counselor. I didn't want to go, but I knew I couldn't get out of it. I just had to play along to his delusion that I was the sole reason we were both unhappy.

The meeting with Mr. Peterson was not a private one on one session with me; it was with both of us. I was not comfortable knowing that I'm going to be asked to be honest and say how I felt about Max; with him sitting next to me.

While I don't recall the questions, I was asked or my responses from that single session. I do remember Mr. Peterson was quick to notice that I had already mentally checked out from our marriage. He saw that it was Max's insecurities that had caused the wedge in our marriage. Mr. Peterson made Max aware of how I had been impacted over the last few years.

Max was warned to tread carefully before making any more accusations; Max didn't realize that it was his actions that were causing him to lose me. I had confirmed that was the case, and that I was barely hanging on. That was an eye-opening session for Max to hear from a trusted, neutral party as to what was going on.

I received an apology with promises of change to his behavior and his attitude toward me.

While I was quite confident that I still wanted to end things, I did see a small glimmer of hope. I felt that I owed it to Max to allow him the chance to make good on his promises. All of Max's attempts at changing were short lived. A few months had passed, and he went right back to allowing his jealousy and insecurities get the better of him. He had begun intentionally provoking arguments with me. Max felt that our marriage was inadequate because we never fought.

He learned that from watching his parents that fought all of the time. Max's father told him years ago that all couples argue, it was normal. I tried to explain that this behavior is not normal; it was stressful, exhausting and pushing me away. Disagreements or having a different opinion are typical; while provoking your spouse to bring them to tears was not natural, loving, or healthy behavior.

Max had a hard time taking advice from me; I had come from a broken home with no parents raising me. In his mind, I didn't have credibility on this matter. It went against everything he knew to be "normal" behavior between spouses.

I had been playing a particular MMORPG for a few months at this point. This game has a real cash economy attached to it. The idea is that you create your avatar and you can learn a variety of skills to help you hunt, craft, and mine. There are a few players that are heavily invested and have made large sums of money. There is so much to this MMORPG, so I'll keep it as brief as possible.

Anyone from anywhere can create an avatar, you will see these avatars running around this vast universe, and you can interact with them. There is an option to start a society or join an existing one, and you can kill enemies and loot goodies that range in value. You can communicate with other players if you choose or you can decline to speak to anyone. Your avatar has a wide range of commands that can make them dance, whistle, wave, laugh, buy, sell, trade, and show enthusiasm. You get the idea.

Anyway, I found this to be interesting as I had never played a game of this nature before. As with any game of this nature, you will meet other players. Sometimes it's a quick question like, "Where's the nearest teleporter?" Other times you get chatting with another player and realize you've just made an in-game friend that you can request a friendship. So, when your friend is logged in, you can see that they are on. It makes it easy to talk to them without having to run around the vast land areas hoping you'll bump into them again.

With that said, I had made such an acquaintance while running from one teleporter to the next. The area I had found myself in was an area I didn't have any business being in that area. My avatar was new, no armor, no weapons, and the enemies were too strong, and I kept dying. Each time my avatar revived; I noticed that another avatar is also reviving in the same spot.

We had starting chatting and realized we were on the same mission; turns out that we had the same idea. We decided to help each other out, and we chatted along the way. This avatar was male and was being played by a male in England. He was just as new to this as I was and we had become in-game friends.

I was excited that I had finally made it to the teleporter after many failed attempts. I decided to share my small victory with Max and tell the story of how it happened. Max was not impressed. He ignored my excitement and focused on the fact that I was talking with a guy from England.

Max had felt that I was spending too much time playing and he thought that my behavior was rude. He had made dinner, and I was expected to sit with him while we ate. I was itching to get back to finish what I was doing. I was in the middle of helping my in-game friend. Max had expressed his opinion; which was that I had become addicted.

In reality; I would log in around 4:00 pm and play until 9:00 pm or maybe 10:00 pm. Yes, I would have enjoyed my meals at the computer, I was not addicted. I had found a hobby to keep me busy, seems I was not allowed to have any interests that didn't include Max. I was meeting people and my time spent in-game was time away from Max.

He was free to come and go as he pleased or spend time with whomever he wanted whenever he wanted. I never gave it a second thought because I trusted him. Max never trusted me to spend time with others that he could not approve of himself. I'm not sure what triggered his insecurity.

He felt so strongly that I was an addict that he told his mother, Linda and best friend, Lou just how awful I was treating him, and he felt unappreciated. Linda knew he was overreacting, and she thought that Max was out of line. My mother-in-law had called to tell me that she stuck up for me during her conversation with Max.

Linda knew that I wasn't the cheating type, she recalled the heartache that Max had caused me when we were dating in our teenage years. Linda was referring to the multiple times Max would call things off, then realize that he wanted me around, which lasted a month or two before the cycle started over again. Max was always the one to break things off and ask for forgiveness.

Linda had apologized on his behalf and thanked me for being such a good friend to Max and not giving up on him back then. She recognized the toll his actions were taking on me. I think she was afraid that one day I wouldn't be so forgiving.

Lou on the other hand, fed into Max's insecurity and planted the seed that maybe he should play too, you know to keep an eye on me. Lou, the same guy that professed his love for me a few times while he was drunk. Lou, the same guy that confessed that he had the urge to kiss during a New Year's party at Shelly's house; with Max and his wife Tina in the next room.

For the record, nothing ever happened with Lou. He made a few advances which I had turned down, nor did I ever tell Max or Lou's wife Tina. I wasn't going to be responsible for breaking up a lifelong friendship or a marriage. Lou was doing a good job at calling attention to himself. Tina had caught Lou on a few occasions; passed out at the computer after a night of heavy drinking with chat windows open. Lou had been having inappropriate chat sessions with who he thought were 18-20-year-old college girls.

It was at that point that Max's opinion of this "stupid" game was now interesting enough to start playing. He wanted to keep an eye on who I was talking with and making sure that I was not sharing too much information or being seduced online.

What was something just for me had now been taken over by Max. He had made in game friendships as well, and I didn't share in his jealousy or feel the need to hover while he was typing to them. Max had even joined a society with a group of many players which was an excellent way to share information and organize missions.

This stupid game wasn't so dumb once Max started playing. It wasn't long before Max was eating his meals at his computer and spending a few hours in the evening doing what I had been doing. While I didn't get an apology for his assumptions, he could at least see that someone across the Atlantic Ocean wasn't seducing me.

It had been my experience that anytime one issue had been resolved, there was another one waiting to rear its ugly head. I could not catch a break; I felt that I had to justify myself constantly. I couldn't do what I wanted when I wanted without Max's approval or him inserting himself into every situation. I couldn't spend my money without consulting Max first.

Both of our paychecks were set up as a direct deposit. Max was in charge of the finances. *Something I thought was a good responsibility for him to learn, ended up biting me in the ass.* Max had learned to budget our pooled income and make sure our bills were paid, but as with most things came a double standard. What was okay for Max was not okay for me.

From the money I had been contributing from my full-time job each week, I was given an allowance. Yes, like a teenager that earned $20 each week for mowing the lawn, that is what I was allowed as spending cash.

Meanwhile, Max had a serious "addiction" to buying hockey cards, thanks to Lou. Max and Lou would go out each weekend and spend $30, $45, $60, $80 a week on hockey cards. Those two gamblers were hoping they would find a rare gem or a card that had an autograph or jersey that would be worth what they had just spent.

The friendship between Max and Lou was not your typical friendship. They had become codependent and always competed to keep up with the lifestyle that the other had. When Lou bought the latest and greatest new shiny thing, Max did the same. They went back and forth in that manner since they were kids. It was as if neither Lou or Max were completely happy in their own lives and were jealous of what the other one had. They were (and I bet still are) always trying to one-up each other.

Not only did Max spend an obscene amount of our money on hockey cards, but he also enjoyed a case of beer and hard liquor every weekend. His justification was that he accounted for the beer in the budget. During the weeks that he'd spend more than he should have, he didn't take less the following week. I was given less or sometimes nothing extra because "we" couldn't afford it. Max had suggested that I should have budgeted my money better. There was always money for hockey cards and beer, the beer that only he drank.

That's great that he accounted for his hobbies and extracurricular activities, but what about me? How was that fair?

Max spent our money any way he wanted to, but I was given $20 a week (if I was lucky) and needed his permission if I wanted to go out for lunch instead of going home to eat. It's not like I had any high maintenance rituals or hobbies of my own that I was spending my money on. I was using my money for snacks and drinks, or sometimes lunch for myself while I was at work.

I had approached Max with my concerns with how he was budgeting our joint earnings, and how I couldn't help but notice he was spending more than he should. Max told me that he could rework the budget so that I could get a bit more, but that would result in one of the bills not getting paid. I could get a second job, that was his solution. Max was not willing to compromise his hockey card/beer fund.

I tried to avoid going home for lunch because I didn't want to run into him during my one hour of peace. By this time we had our house to ourselves. I suspect that his behavior had also been something he learned from his parents. His father, Jack worked to provide for their family, his check was deposited, and Linda took care of the bills and spending. Anytime Jack spent money; it resulted in a power struggle that led to an argument.

I had decided that I was going to save my "allowance" and put it into my savings account. I had started eating at home in the mornings and afternoons in my attempt at budgeting my money. When I came home with a few new articles of clothes (nothing high end or designer) I was confronted as to where I got the money for them. Max was now aware that I had been setting my money aside and suggested that it would be nice if I could contribute a bit to our joint account, seems we might be short paying our car insurance this month.

I was furious! My money was not at all my money, he wanted everything and didn't think he should compromise his selfish needs for the greater good. I told Max that I would not transfer money to cover the car insurance. He needed to do a bit of sacrificing and lay off from buying hockey cards and beer for the rest of the month. He was in charge of the budget, and it was his fault that he had overspent.

Somehow, I was the selfish party; I wasn't contributing enough toward our joint expenses. *My entire check was directly deposited.* The fact that Max brought home a bit more each week and earned a slightly larger commission is what he had based his argument on.

Max was the only employee, so he saw more of his earnings. My commission was based on more than just my sales. Mine was based on a percentage of the sales/losses/expenses from the employees in my department. Our health and dental insurance was deducted from my checks each week, not from his. We were essentially making the same amount each week. How could he say that I was not contributing as much as he was? I certainly wasn't spending as much as he was.

Fast forward a few months because nothing had changed with the exception that Jack was staying with us again. His attempt to reconcile with Linda didn't turn out as he had hoped.

I had made another in-game friend that was going through a less than happy marriage of his own. It was nice to have someone to talk to about this, and it helped me to know that I wasn't crazy. I didn't have anybody to turn to for advice on this matter. The conversations that I had with my new friend from Sweden were a breath of fresh air, considering all of the stress and nonsense I was being forced to endure at home.

Due to the time difference between me in New England and Oscar all the way over in Sweden, we tried to coordinate a time on the weekend to log in. Sometimes we hunted, or we ran new players to some of the teleporters, and sometimes we'd meet up at the Art Gallery in-game and talk about anything, no different than what most friends do in real life.

Max didn't like the idea that I would wake up early (5:00 am) some mornings to talk to Oscar so we could coordinate a time to log in later. It had got to a point where I stopped caring about what Max liked or what might upset him. I was tired of the fighting, his jealousy, my sacrifices to keep the peace and always walking on eggshells in my own home. What I felt I was that I should be allowed to have a friend that I didn't meet through Max. I should be allowed to socialize and have other interests; besides the ones that Max pushed on me. If Max has a problem, then it was merely, his problem. I was tired of putting my happiness on hold because he was uncomfortable. If Max couldn't believe what I was telling him by now, or if he couldn't trust that I was not looking to meet someone new to replace him, that was no longer my concern. I was done!

I had proven to be a loyal, dependable, honest, and equal partner in this marriage. I don't know how else to prove that, and I was exhausted from trying to show him that over the last seven years. I realized that Max wasn't going to change, but I knew something needed too.

Upon considering my options and reflecting on past events that had lead up to this point; I had a few eye-opening moments. As much as Max professed his love, he hinted several times that I'd be prettier if I wore makeup, skirts, dresses, high heels like other women. He'd suggested years ago that I should consider cosmetic surgery to enhance my breast size and to straighten my teeth. These suggestions were coming from a man with a chipped front tooth who is less than average height, wearing shorts year-round because it's hard to find pants in a size 40W/30L.

It was that moment I knew that Max didn't love me for me. He loved the idea of me; I just needed to look like the former neighbor that he had a crush on. His dream girl who was also Tina's older sister. I was the sweet girl you brought home to your parents, the funny, loyal friend, the girlfriend that your family accepted right away. The friend you could be yourself with, no judgments or strings attached.

While his dream girl was the typical girly girl that wore miniskirts, makeup, did her nails and wore high heels. I'm sure she had other great qualities, I didn't know her all that well. This dream girl was in a long-term relationship with one of Max's best friends. This same girl that always kept Max in the friend zone.

I couldn't live like this anymore. I had been unhappy for so long, and I owed it to myself to be happy considering all that I have been through up to this point. Max wouldn't let me go that easily, I needed to escape, but how? Did I have a place to go temporarily? I didn't have enough money to move out on my own yet. Max was successful at keeping me isolated to only having contact with his family and friends. I felt like a prisoner in my own home.

Those thoughts and questions had been playing on repeat in my head for a while before I remembered a conversation that Max and I had a few years ago. I don't recall how the topic came up, but Max thought it was a good idea to talk about how we should handle a divorce, should we end up down that road.

I thought it was odd, but I played along. Max seemed confident that he would be able to forgive just about anything and would be willing to work through any situation, except cheating. I agreed that I felt that would be true for me as well. He went on to say that he thought that we could be civil and hopefully stay friends.

I knew what I had to do! No, no, I didn't cheat, I'm not that kind of girl. I had to make him think I had cheated; it was the only way he would let me go. I called Joey to let him know what my intentions were and asked if I could stay with him and his wife until I get back on my feet. Joey was happy to support me in whichever way I needed; he knew I wasn't happy anymore. With Joey willing to help me; I needed to work on getting out unnoticed.

I know this sounds horrible, but at that moment I didn't see any other option. Trust me; this is not one of my finer moments; it was not a proud moment by any means. I was ashamed that I couldn't make my marriage work. I felt like a loser, and the fact that I was going to have to admit I was divorced did not sit well with me for a long time. I felt like a failure. Those that I loved either left me or they abused me in some way. I was tired of the abuse and needed to help myself out of this situation.

The plan for my great escape took a few weeks to cultivate. I had to coordinate with Joey to make sure he was available to help me on the day that I needed him. I let my boss know of my situation and requested a transfer to one of our sister dealerships; preferably a location that Max didn't show up on a weekly basis. My co-workers knew of my plan, and when Max's work van would pull in, I was alerted, so I didn't have to deal with him directly.

I had to contact our bank and redirect my paychecks into my new checking account. I made sure that my essential paperwork was organized and easily accessible.

I had made sure to wash all of my laundry. In the kitchenette upstairs there was a small open closet that I hid my suitcase. I slowly started packing the clothes that I intended to take with me as not to raise suspicion.

I copied any important documents from my computer onto a USB drive. I packed a few towels and bought new toothbrush and toiletries and put them in my suitcase. I needed to keep my original items in place, as to not raise questions. The idea was to leave without him knowing, nor did I want to be caught in the act.

Max kept the same delivery schedule each week. Max was also a creature of habit. I knew when he left for work, and I knew that Max always came home to use the bathroom before going out on his deliveries. The day his deliveries took him an hour out of town was the day I was waiting for.

That day had arrived, and I had to play it off that I was going to work as I was expected too. Max didn't know that I was waiting to be transferred and my coworkers were happy to cover for me. I drove to "work" and parked in my usual spot, just trying to keep up with appearances. I had to wait about thirty minutes before Max would leave for work before moving my car to a different location. As I said, I knew Max would go home to use the bathroom before starting his deliveries.

I parked my car down the street one block over and walked to the house, locking the door behind me. I heard Max pull into the driveway followed by the sound of the van door closing. I hid upstairs in the kitchenette, knowing that he never went in there. The waiting was killing me. I was so nervous about getting caught. I was having second thoughts about whether I was doing the right thing. The ball was already in motion. Joey is supposed to meet me here any minute.

I hope they don't run into each other as Max is leaving. I hope the cats don't give me away. For the love of god! What was taking Max so long?... Why is he on the phone with Lou? Doesn't he do any work, slacker? Sounds like he's getting ready to leave. Twenty minutes must have passed. Finally!

It sounds like Max is leaving; I can hear the van running. There he goes, the driveway is clear. I make my way downstairs and grab my paperwork from the filing cabinet. I start unplugging my computer and trying to remember which cable goes where. *Oh god, was that the sound of a car door?*

Thank goodness, it's only Joey. I went over my plan with him and let him know how he could help. Joey finishes up with my computer while I bring my car into the driveway. Joey helped to pack up my car, while I took a final look to make sure I had the essentials. I was gone within forty minutes of Max leaving. Feeling confident that I had made a successful escape.

I decided that I owed Max an explanation at the very least. A few nights leading up to this, I decided to write him a letter that ended up being about five pages before I was finished. I left that on his computer and assumed he'd find it once he noticed my computer was missing.

This was the one chance that Max would listen to my side and he couldn't manipulate what I said. My words were right there in front of him. I told him how I had been unhappy for a while and what had caused me to drift further away. I wanted a divorce; I did not want to reconcile or get back together. Please do not try to find me; I didn't want to see him. I was very clear about my intentions. I had to fabricate my cheating story in hopes that it would be the final nail in the coffin.

The letter had mentioned that I would coordinate a day/time to pick up more of my belongings when I was ready to deal with him. He can keep the house and his car that was in my name (*it was almost paid off*). P.S. I took half of what was in the bank account, *I figured that was fair. I wasn't trying to ruin his life; I just wanted to get out.*

I ended up staying with Joey and his wife for five months until I was able to find an apartment that I could afford. I was grateful they offered a place to stay in my time of desperation. On a positive note, I was transferred to another dealership close to where my new apartment was. There was no chance of running into Max.

I was beginning to have mixed feelings about the thought of living by myself. While most young adults look forward to that moment, and in some cases, it's treated as a rite of passage. I didn't want to impose any more than I felt that I had on Joey and his wife, who just had a newborn son.

While I had been responsible for myself and maintained a sense of independence, it dawned on me that I would need to do everything on my own. It was scary which brought on anxiety, and self-doubt also made an appearance. Even the process of talking with potential landlords and property managers was uncomfortable; I'm sure that they sensed the desperation in my voice.

Once I had been approved for my first apartment, it was time to coordinate another move. I rented a small box truck to pick up more of my belongings from my former house, which meant I had to deal with Max on his terms. I enlisted Joey to help me move, drive the box truck and act as my security detail because I didn't know what to expect from Max.

Max had changed the locks and felt that he couldn't trust me. He didn't want me going back while he wasn't there to make sure I didn't take what wasn't mine. I left him my car that I could have had repossessed; I left him the house and didn't want anything to do with it. I packed my essential belongings and didn't care about the material things that I could buy later. I only took out half of what was in our joint checking account when I could have cleaned it out just out of spite. But I'm not that person. I certainly didn't want any of his hockey cards.

Max still showing that he never did trust me and this his way of trying to control my actions. I was not going to allow him to control me anymore!

While I'm walking through the house with Max as my shadow; I happened to notice a vase of red roses on the kitchen table, with a card that was in Max's handwriting, professing his love for another woman. I was not jealous; I'm the one that broke things off. I was surprised with how quickly he had moved on. It had been five months, and he had moved his girlfriend into the house.

Meanwhile, I'm being asked what I was looking for, that there was nothing of mine in this room or that room. It seems that Max had moved most of my things to one location upstairs in what used to be our bedroom. Max claimed that he was deeply offended in how I chose to leave that he couldn't stand to be in that room anymore. Max also didn't like my portrayal of him in my letter as the bad guy.

Max was so hurt that he had already moved on and was sharing his bed with another woman within five months of me leaving our seven-year relationship. Perhaps he was reflecting his affair when he was accusing me of cheating. No, Max was in no way the bad guy. Clearly, I was being unreasonable. What a jackass! I think since he wasn't getting the attention he wanted from me, he found it elsewhere. He may choose to live with blinders on, but I could see right through him.

A few months had passed when I get an email from Max, and he wants me to come by and pick up my belongings that I do not wish to have thrown away. It was suggested that I bring friends because he wasn't going to help me. I made last minute arrangement with two former co-workers that I knew had a truck to help me move a few larger pieces.

I arrive, and Max greets me on the front porch. I can see that most of his family is in the house. *This situation was about to get very uncomfortable.* The one item I wanted was my corner curio cabinet that was in the living room with the french doors. The same room his family was occupying. If I had to guess, Max must have told them not to talk to me or offer to help me move my things. It would be the only explanation for them to respond the way that they did.

While I entered the room, I didn't get glares of anger, but looks of sadness. They were watching TV while I was carefully packing my trinkets and wrapping the glass shelves. I felt like all of their eyes were staring at the back of my head. There were a few odds and ends that I grabbed while Max insists on following me around the house.

I'm having a hard time going back into the living room as I'm beginning to feel like a sad dog with its tail between its leg. It was all that I could do from holding back the tears. I felt like I had disappointed them in some way. Shelly had pulled me aside while Max was in the bathroom, she let me know that she doesn't agree with what Max is doing or how he's treating me, then hugged me.

I'm not sure why this bothers me so much. Could it be a sense of shame on my part? I didn't like feeling as if I had given up; I wasn't a quitter. Was I hoping for his family to stick up for me and stand up to Max? Was I picking up on their sadness of me leaving? Had Max planned this intentionally to make me feel worse than I already had?

I'd like to think that they weren't on board with what Max had done, but they were living there now and didn't want to rock the boat. I wouldn't find it hard to believe that Max gave them an ultimatum like that. What I do know is that it still hurts and I feel like his family saw the signs and didn't do anything. Leaves me feeling let down by my family that didn't want to get involved or speaks up on my behalf.

There were a few more times in which I received an email from Max with an ultimatum attached. Max had a knack for forcing things to go his way while I paid out unnecessarily. I suspect this was his attempt to hurt me and to put a strain on my wallet. Not only was I harassed by Max but his now fiancée, Penny who's as crazy and delusional as Max.

One evening I was asked to stop by to pick up something. I was met at the front steps by Penny. She was expecting me and confirmed who I was, and she also made it clear that I was not welcome in **her** house. I had caused too much disruption, and she didn't want me coming around anymore.

What? Are you serious? I'm being asked to stop by, and this is **not** your house. My name is still on it, and I have more of a right to be here than you do!

Penny was accusing me of wanting to get back together with Max, and that she's with him now and how much happier he is since I left. I reminded her that I was the one that left him and I had no intention of getting back together with Max. I left, I filed for divorce, I kept my new apartment a secret from him on purpose. Does that sound like a person that wants to reconcile? Max is your problem now. From the sounds of things, you two deserve each other.

This heated discussion continued for a good five minutes before Max made an appearance. *How nice of him to sick his nasty fiancée on me just to start an argument in the front yard.* "Hey, I see you've met Penny, oh and this is why I asked you to stop by" as he hands me a small moving box with contents unknown. *Unknown because I wasn't sticking around to sift through it with Cujo foaming at the mouth.*

I went back to my car to leave, and Max's younger brother, Shawn stopped me. Shawn noticed it was me and wanted to say hi. Penny and Max are yelling at him to leave me alone, and not to talk to me. His brother hopped in the passenger side, and I drove up the street a bit to finish talking to him. I was trying to calm down as I found Max and Penny's behavior to be upsetting.
He goes on to tell me that he and his girlfriend, Heather are still dating. Penny is Heather's aunt. That's how she met Max and realized she could capitalize on his situation. Shawn mentioned that I wasn't gone two months before Max started dating Penny and asked her to move in. He couldn't believe how stupid Max was for treating me the way he had. No matter what, he would always consider me his sister, then he hugged me before leaving my car.

I did leave with whatever it was that he wanted me to pick up. Oh! I remember it was our wedding photo album and pictures from our honeymoon. When I got home, I went through them one last time before feeding them into my paper shredder. I was done with that part of my life (divorce pending), and I didn't want any reminders from it lingering around.

Speaking of the divorce, that day had arrived. By this time, almost one year had passed since our separation and Max, and I were able to be civil. We had to pass through security, and we had been asked what our business was at the courthouse; the security guard had commented that we were the calmest couple looking to get divorced, almost too happy to be there.

We did have time to sort out the details and going forward we agreed to be civil. Some papers needed to be filled out before going in front of the judge. One of which asked if I wanted to resume my maiden name or if I had planned on keeping it the same.

I preferred to keep it the same, so I didn't have to change my name on everything all over again. Max spoke up and practically demanded that I change my last name back. He didn't want me keeping his name if I wasn't his wife, nor did he want his future wife sharing the same last name as his ex-wife.

I could not believe what I was hearing! Blindsided again! We are getting divorced, and he no longer has a say in decisions that affect me. Who does he think he is, trying to control my actions or my last name?

Max insisted that I change my last name or I could look at another ultimatum. While filling out the paperwork, there was a space to write in the name I wanted to use as my legal last name. I was stumped, my maiden name belonged to

Joey's father, a last name that wasn't mine to begin with. Should I use my original last name at birth?

Upon reading the document closer, I learned that I **"could choose"** to change my last name and had a few weeks to fill out the respective form to confirm the change. I put my last name at birth down to appease Max, but I had no intention of following through on the next step. Touché! *That was a small victory for me.*

It felt great to be free and out from Max's grasp. My conscience was now clear that I could continue to move forward in a new relationship without the guilt that I was technically a married woman.

CHAPTER 6:

Momma Drama

I don't give up easily on someone. If I am pushed to the point of no return; I will leave and never look back." - H. Racine

A new chapter of my life had started. I began to think about my relationship with my mother or in my case a lack thereof. Our mother-daughter relationship had been one continuous roller coaster ride. My mother was around for the first nine years of my life and pretty much absent for the next thirty years with brief appearances and a handful of phone calls in between.

The thought of my mother brings up mixed feelings. There is a part of me that recognizes that she was dealt a crappy hand; while another part is still disappointed with her constant poor judgment. I know that in her mind she will defend that did the best that she could for us. There is a part of me that thinks that she can't be serious.

While my mother was secretly visiting George in prison, she was acquainted with George's cellmate, Gerald. Do I need to mention that Gerald was also in for the same crime against his daughter?

Any theories as to who my mother started her next relationship with? She's all too predictable; no guesses are needed.

During the time that Max and I were planning our wedding; I decided to call and extend the invitation to only her. My mother wanted to know why Gerald was not invited. She felt that it was rude of me not to extend an invitation to him. He was my stepfather after all. I kid you not, those were her words to me.

I was fully grown, practically raised myself without a father figure, I sure as hell didn't need or want him in my life.

My reply to her was that "I could not in good conscience allow a man who was in prison for sexually abusing his daughter around the small children that would also be attending our wedding. There was no way I would be comfortable knowing that he's there. How can you even think that it's acceptable?"

Oh, Wait! She is the same woman that wanted to put locks on the inside of the doors with my abuser under the same roof. Shame on me for thinking she had a different outlook.

My mother went on to tell me that Gerald had served his time and that I should give him a chance, and everyone deserves a second chance. *I am on board with offering second chances, but never to pedophiles.* She felt that I was overreacting. I'd rather overreact to this situation knowing I was doing everything in my power to protect those kids than to sweep it under the rug and turn a blind eye on a known sexual predator.

Just when I thought my mother couldn't disappoint me any more than she already had; she decided that if Gerald wasn't invited to our wedding, then she wasn't going either. Not only was it her choice not to attend my wedding, but she's just thinking about her happiness and is all too willing to put me back in danger. *That is a pain that I don't think will ever go away.*

I did my part to extend the invitation to my mother. It was my mistake to assume that she would jump at the chance to see her daughter get married since she had missed out on so much of my life. Shame on me for thinking that she ever had my best interest in mind.

As long as my mother was going to continue to stay with Gerald, I could not be associated with her. I didn't see any other way around that. She kept those blinders on, and she could not understand why I was so harsh, and she even made the comment that she didn't raise me that way.

To which I reminded her that she didn't raise me at all, she left after nine years. That was it, almost five years would pass before I would try and reconcile with her.

At this point, I was thirty years old, and I had started to think about if I had kids. I had hoped that I would have a better relationship with them. It had dawned on me that my mother was a grandmother and had yet to meet her grandchildren.

I had been thinking long and hard about if I wanted to reconcile with my mother. I put myself in her shoes, and I felt sad for her. That was not what I wanted for myself. I wanted a better relationship with my kids, should I have any.

Part of me was confident that I would only get hurt again. Another part of me knew it wasn't going to work itself out unless I made an effort. I knew full well my mother would not reach out to me because she didn't see where she had done anything wrong.

I had decided to make one last attempt at salvaging our mother-daughter relationship. I knew that I had to be direct and blunt in explaining how her actions made me feel. Mom had to know how hurt and disappointed I was. This would be my last olive branch. I was serious about cutting her out of my life for good, and it would be unwise for her to test my limits.

We must have talked for at least an hour. The conversation was very emotional (lots of crying on both ends). It was important for me to tell her how I felt because I knew she would not recognize it on her own. In some ways, I feel like the parent guiding her, and she's the child learning what is acceptable behavior and learning how her actions have consequences.

My mother would play the victim, and how she was hurt and forced to make tough choices. While she may have been a victim during her youth and to the harsh discipline of her parents, she was not a victim when it came to her choices about her kids. She has never made that connection. She assumed that when we were eighteen, we'd run back to her and be a happy family. That day never happened.

Now that my mother knew that Joey was now married with kids of his own, she'd try to pry information out of me as to where he was or how can she get in touch with him. I knew better than to give her that information. I knew Joey wasn't ready to see her, nor did he have any intention of letting our mother back into his life or around his kids.

I had tried to explain how Joey felt as delicately as possible, but as usual, she refused to own any responsibility. My mother could not understand what she did that was so horrible that Joey wouldn't want to see her. Our mother was remembering the little boy crying in the back seat that wanted to come home so badly. In her mind she hadn't done anything since then to anger him, so why was he upset? Joey is now a grown man with a family, and he's had time to reflect on past events. I had suggested that Joey is probably looking for an apology and an explanation.

Just because I had made my choice to open the line of communication with her, doesn't mean Joey had reached that stage in his life. Our mother just could not comprehend what she needed to apologize for. She still insists on sticking with the "I did the best that I could for you kids and Child Services made me give up my parental rights." justification.

If our mother honestly felt that she had done her best, then why did she lie for years to our extended family? I suspect that grandma Gina thought it was the best way to handle that shame. We may have had other family members that could have helped us. Grandma Gina was always looking out for herself and kept sweeping things under the rug. She was so afraid of the truth.

Whenever there was a family reunion, our mother was asked where her kids were. It seems Hannah and Joey were often at summer camp or spending time with friends *(for nine years in a row)*. I suspect that we were never brought over during our weekend visits because the truth might come out as to what had really happened. *The web of lies would unravel, then how would our family look? That is what I suspect grandma Gina was worried about.*

While Hannah and Joey were forgotten members of the family, good ole' Gerald had taken our place. It just occurred to me that Gerald had attended multiple family functions, he was the newest (3rd) husband. I shudder to think that he had plenty of opportunities to put his filthy hands on one of my cousins.

How could grandma Gina and my mother think that bringing a pedophile into the family was a good idea? It wasn't smart of them to pass a wolf off in sheep's clothing while placing the safety of the other kids in our family at risk.

I just don't understand their thought process and why they both insist on making the same mistakes over and over again.

Not only was Gerald the newest family member, a known former prisoner for sexual abuse toward a minor, but grandma Gina allowed them to rent the two rooms in the attic when my mother was "forced" out from her apartment.

So taking in her grandchildren to protect them from a predator was not an option. Her innocent grandchildren were split up and forgotten by the family. Allowing the cellmate of my abuser to live under her roof was apparently the better choice in her twisted mind. Thanks, grandma Gina for always looking out.

While I chose to salvage the relationship with my mother, I did not extend that same kindness to grandma Gina. When I was eighteen, grandma Gina offered to sell me her old car. She was getting a newer vehicle and thought it was a nice gesture to pass down her old one to her granddaughter.

This was the first and last good deed she offered to me. While I was in the process of talking with her about getting the car insured, applying for new license plates and getting the title transferred; I could tell that this deal was going south fast. In typical grandma Gina style, she knew exactly how this process works and which steps needed to be done and in which order. She never gives anything without strings attached or telling you what do to with her item.

I had attempted to correct her (shame on me) because I had been working in a dealership long enough to know how the process worked and her thinking was not correct. Grandma Gina took my action to educate her as a sign of disrespect, and I was no longer worthy of her used car. She'd rather send it to the junkyard than for me (her ungrateful, smart-mouthed granddaughter) to have it.

I was recruited to help my mother move out from the attic to an apartment with Gerald. At this time I had my little truck and didn't mind helping. My grandmother arrived as I was helping my mother move out when she pulled my mother aside to tell her that she didn't appreciate having strangers in her home.

I was referred to as a stranger. *What the hell is wrong with her?* That was the moment that I disowned her. Grandma Gina was dead to me. This is something that I have made peace with, and I don't feel guilty about my decision to cut her out. Grandma Gina had shown her true self at that moment. It was a side that I had only heard stories about. We had never formed a bond, so leaving her behind was not at all a loss in my life. I was never a priority in her life, to begin with.

I have learned that it's okay to make the tough choice to cut out the family member(s) that only bring stress and negativity into your life. A family is not just those related to you by blood, but it also applies to those friends that have seen you through everything and continue to support you. Those friends that share in your successes and remain in your corner to cheer you on. Somehow the abuse I endured as a young child had caused the family shame (as far as grandma Gina was concerned), and I had been cast out.

It would be fourteen years before I would see my grandmother again.

As for my mother, the line of communication has remained open since 2008. We talk on the phone occasionally, but most of our conversations take place on Facebook. Since I now live over seven hours away, I don't see her as often as **she'd** like. I am perfectly content with our long-distance relationship.

My mother has been an excellent resource for finding out about our family medical history, which gets scarier every time something new gets added to the list.

Medical concerns such as Heart failure/Heart attacks, High Blood Pressure, Hemochromatosis (blood rich in iron), Scoliosis, Fatty Non-Alcoholic Liver Cirrhosis, Skin Psoriasis, Cancer, Early onset of menopause (starts at 40 and lasts ten years), and my personal favorite, Dementia (Alzheimer's). This list is just from my mother's side of the family.

As far as my mother is concerned, she still sees me as her nine-year-old little girl. Maybe she's trying to make up for lost time. The tone of nurturing mom comes through in many conversations and posts on social media. I might share with her a choice that I made as a means of filling her in, and I get an "I fully support your choice, no matter what" response. I wasn't asking for her approval; my choice was made, that is what's new with me. I choose not to respond in a way that might hurt her feelings.

I can only handle my mother in small doses. I don't share her interest in visiting for a weekend or taking part in mother-daughter activities. While I may have forgiven her, I can't trust her, nor will I ever forget what she's put me through. I've spent a good portion of my life feeling embarrassed and ashamed to admit that she is, in fact, my mother. I tell her that I love her at the end of our conversations, but that is for her benefit, and I feel it's something that I am expected to say.

I do care about her well-being, and there is a part of me that feels like I need to look out for her because she can't look out for herself. I recognized that she was in a similar marriage with Gerald that I was in with Max. Gerald was just as smothering, hovering, wanting to know who she was talking too and keeping track of how long she was talking on the phone. He had made her feel that she was worthless and only he could love her.

Many of you might feel that my mom is getting what she deserves, and I understand that. I know that my safety was not her top priority, and she gave up on me. I am not my mother. I can't sit back and watch this ship sink. She may have chosen to save herself during my trauma, but I can't in good conscience watch her drown without throwing her a life preserver. It was her now choice to sink or swim to safety.

Mom chose to swim. She realized that I was right about Gerald and her eyes were now open as to what he was doing and that she didn't have to put up with that abuse. As with many spouses that are in emotionally abusive relationships, they are made to feel that no one else will love them or put up with them.

The abuser will work hard to isolate their partner from their family. The abusers are often very charming as a means of attracting their mate and getting close to their family. They work their charm and use their sense of humor as a decoy to distract from the elaborate scheme they have worked up.

I have worked very hard to not be like my mother. The thought of me falling into the same poor choices scares me. My mother was never a role model in my eyes. She represented everything I did not want to become if I was a parent.

The idea of me having kids didn't sit well with me. Not that I don't like kids, I'm a natural when it comes to kids. My family history of abuse runs strong, and I was afraid that my child would to go through the same trauma that I had endured. The cycle of abuse needs to stop with me, and I have made every effort to make sure that it does.

If you are wondering if my mother knows that I've written a book, the answer is YES. I thought it was better that she heard it from me directly than to hear about it from someone else. My mother understands that this is part of my healing process and she supports my choice. I wasn't seeking her approval. I expect that if my mother does read this, her feelings will be hurt. I cannot be held accountable for the choices that were made on my behalf.

My mother and I were never close nor do I expect that we will ever share a special bond. Part of my healing process includes seeking closure with my mother whether that means keeping the line of communication open or cutting her out. I have made peace with both options. My mother no longer has any control over me, and that is a huge part of moving forward from the pain that she has inflicted. I can forgive her for her poor choices because that is what I needed to do to release any of the negative feelings I was harboring.

I don't see us moving beyond our current long-distance relationship. Honestly, I'm content with that arrangement.

CHAPTER 7:

Full of Second Chances

"If you have been brutally broken, but still have the courage to be gentle to others, then you deserve a love deeper than the ocean itself." - Nikita Gill

By April of 2007, I was living by myself in my tiny one-bedroom apartment. It was scary and liberating at the same time. Nobody was waiting to use the bathroom while I was taking a shower. I wouldn't get a game of twenty questions if I didn't get home at 5:15 pm on the dot. No more accusations or being dragged to band practice. I finally had a quiet place to myself!

Since I didn't have hovering eyes over my shoulder, I resumed my online gaming. When I did log back in, Oscar wanted to make sure that it was actually me and not Max posing as me. Oscar started asking questions that only I would know the answer to. My in-game relationship with Oscar had developed into a great friendship. Even to this day, Oscar has always been one of my biggest supporters.

A few of my in-game friendships grew into real-life friendship, one of those friendships developed into a romantic relationship. I realize that many people will have a hard time believing that a romance that starts online could work out. I'm happy to prove the skeptics wrong and let you know that we are celebrating our ten-year wedding anniversary in November of this year.

How is that possible? With mutual trust, respect and technology like webcams, Skype and instant messenger. Jay and I developed our friendship for a good six months before we were ready to meet in person. If Jay and I weren't spending time in-game, then we were chatting through messenger or trying to coordinate watching the same movie over Skype until one of us went to bed.

Jay and I coordinated a week in the summer for him to come down to visit me. I was excited and a bit nervous as the day of his arrival grew closer. The nervousness went away and was replaced with a sense of comfort. This was all very new to me. I had never been in a position to entertain a guest before.

Our first face to face encounter had gone so well that we had become engaged almost ten months later. Seven months after that, our marriage ceremony took place in my tiny apartment. We had to continue our long-distance marriage over the next year while I was in the process of moving to Canada as a permanent resident.

My relationship with Jay was very different from my relationship with Max. I could be myself with Jay, and he actively listened to my concerns. I voiced my interests and Jay would encourage me to do what makes me happy while being genuinely interested in what I had to say.

I was used to Max shooting down my ideas and hobbies as being stupid, or they were a waste of money. I wasn't allowed to have interests of my own with Max. My feelings and concerns weren't valid.

What Max wanted to change about me, Jay complimented and embraced. I was finally being seen for who I was. I wasn't being controlled, manipulated or discarded. I had been given a second chance at marriage, love, and happiness. Jay knew there would be emotional baggage that will follow me into our relationship. He has been very patient with me and has offered to help as I've been slowly unpacking and sort through my shortcomings.

Finding work in Canada proved to be a little harder than I had expected. Many lines of work require special certificates or proof of an apprenticeship. I had bounced from a few automotive businesses and dealerships during the first few years.

Having spent my almost fifteen years in this industry, I had realized that it was time for a career change. I was great at my job, but I was never passionate about my line of work. I loved my co-workers back home and enjoyed the friends that I made out in Alberta, but things were different in Ontario. I had a hard time finding where I fit in. Besides, it was never my intention of becoming a Parts Manager. I was no longer being challenged, and it was time for me to explore my options.

With encouragement and support from Jay, I made the switch. My artistic side needed an outlet. I had become quite proficient as a cake decorator, and I enjoyed baking, so why not give that a try?

Becoming a cake decorator had been my dream job since I was a young girl. I remember walking past the bakery department at the local grocery store and stopping to watch the employee decorate a cake through the customer viewing area.

It was that moment when I realized that an artist didn't have to use canvas and paint as their only means of expression. An artist had multiple mediums to express their creativity.

I had signed myself up for the Wilton Cake Decorating classes, which I enjoyed. The practice cakes were brought in to work the next day, and it wasn't long before I became the "Go To" person for my co-workers that wanted a birthday cake made for their kids. Before I knew it, I was taking custom orders and getting paid for doing something that I loved.

A little encouragement from Jay went a long way. I had proved to myself that I was good enough and could be successful as a cake decorator.

I had an opportunity to make a career change. A change that may not have happened without the support and encouragement from my husband. Thank You, Jay! You've allowed me to experience my dream job which I truly loved.

Why the past tense?

Due to my scoliosis and a former employer pushing me too hard, even ignoring the doctor's note that they insisted I get which explained my limitations. My former employer was unwilling to accommodate me or allow me to work within my means. I was being asked to continue lifting, twisting, reaching and doing all of the things I was not supposed to do.

The temporary light duty restrictions became permanent light duty restrictions. I was bullied by my manager and another associate to work harder, work faster because I didn't "look" sick. I was forced to quit to avoid causing severe damage to my spine.

Luckily Jay was doing very well with his business, and he insisted that I take some time off. He was confident that he would be able to support both of us. Jay also recognized that I had never really had a chance to stop and rest with how my life had been up to this point. I was lucky to get a full week of paid vacation time each year; in most cases, I opted to have that time paid out.

The idea of taking time off and not having to get up so early for the baking shifts sounded very tempting. I've always been the type of person that wants to contribute, and it was this part of me that was having a hard time accepting the help. I knew that I needed the rest to allow my back to heal before I made things worse.

Jay had brought up many good points about me taking time off, and all were very appealing. I had agreed to take some time off to relax. It was during this time that we bought our first house together. Having time off allowed me to help set up our new home. We had everything unpacked and set up within two weeks from moving in.

We finally had the flexibility to be able to travel and take several cruises. If you ever have the chance to take a cruise, GO! *You can thank me later.*

I felt it was time to get back into the workforce last year. I thought I had taken enough time off and my back seemed to be okay. I was hired at the local grocery store as a cake decorator. I loved being back to work and doing what I loved.

I realized that three weeks in, my back could no longer handle it. Even starting out as part-time proved to be too much. I could hardly get through three hours of a four-hour shift without being in excruciating pain.

At least this manager and team were very willing to accommodate my limitations. Due to my inability and restrictions, that means that more than 80% of my duties would fall on my co-workers. It went beyond them reaching a heavy box on the top shelf for me. It would be a total disruption of their duties.

That wasn't fair to them as this wasn't just a temporary workaround situation. Once again, I'm forced to quit a job I love because my back can't handle it. My days off were full days of rest and nothing else.

While my mind is young, my back felt like it was 90-years old, all hunched over, unable to stand straight, barely able to get out of bed the next day. This was not the quality of life that I had envisioned, nor was it something I could allow to continue.

This is a topic I still have a hard time accepting. I don't qualify for government medical assistance because I'm not disabled enough. I can walk unassisted, get myself dressed and I'm not experiencing chronic pain.

I've been seeing a chiropractor once a month for regular adjustments; which is what helps me to stay mobile. I suffer from Lumbar and Thoracic Mechanical Joint Dysfunction which restricts my range of mobility and puts a limit on how much I can lift and move without risking further injury.

You can see my dilemma. My only option appears to be that I work from home where I can make my own hours and take as many breaks as I need. I'm only 5 feet tall, so most things are out of my reach. *Short girl problems, the struggle is real.*

While there are more stories that I could share about the last ten years with my husband. Stories about my immigration process, driving five days from Ontario to Alberta and back again two years later, our memorable wedding ceremony in my tiny apartment and the portobello mushroom incident; but they would not help to move this story along.

I will say that I am grateful to have a partner that loves me for me, a husband that has seen me through my worst times and stands by my side to comfort me and offers to dry my tears while I sort through my emotional baggage.

Jay has been the one constant nurturing person in my life. He reminds me each day that I am loved unconditionally. I could not have asked for a better partner in life.

CHAPTER 8:

No Means No

However you dress, wherever you go, Yes means Yes and No means No." - Dr. Seuss

The phrase "No Means No" is pretty cut and dry for most of us. We all have heard this phrase at one point or another. Maybe your parent had said this to you when you wanted a snack before eating your dinner. Perhaps an older sibling said this to you after you had asked to borrow something of theirs.

I bet it's safe to say that this is not your first time hearing no means no. Just in my own experience; I was taught that when somebody says No, I was to respect that. I was under the impression that when I said NO, that my boundaries would be recognized or any unwanted actions would stop.

There are those people who feel that specific rules don't apply to them.

Here are examples of when my No didn't mean No; along with horrible experiences from medical professionals that seem to fit in this section.

Example 1: All encounters with George that resulted in me being sexually abused. There were countless no's that didn't mean no.

_____

Example 2: My no was ignored when asked about moving to Mrs. Smith's house.

_____

Example 3: When I was sixteen, I was doing what I felt was responsible. I thought that it would be a good idea to start birth control pills. I wasn't sexually active at that time, but I wanted to be prepared. I was also hoping the pills would help regulate my periods because they were far from regular since they started five years prior. Mrs. Smith didn't like the idea; she made a nasty comment how I should keep my legs closed if I didn't want to get pregnant before telling me that I was old enough to make my own appointments. *How nice of her to assume that I intended to sleep around and make me feel ashamed for wanting to protect myself.* I made my appointment for my first gynecologist visit.

The only doctor's office I had been to was a pediatric clinic down the street. They offered to see me since I had been a patient there before and was still a minor. I was advised that I should seek an actual gynecologist in the future. I didn't know what to expect; it's not like I had anyone to talk to about my womanly concerns. Mrs. Smith was clearly not interested.

I did expect an uncomfortable pelvic examination and a Pap test, both of which took place. The nurse had commented that most patients going in for this kind of exam are usually better "groomed." *As if I wasn't embarrassed enough, I was trying not to get emotional, but the tears followed.*

I apologized to her and let her know that I didn't have a woman in my life to coach me through this process. I didn't realize that this visit was going to include a breast exam as well. I was not on board and made it known that I was not comfortable. My no did not mean no in this situation. Not only do I get insulted while I'm in my most vulnerable position, but now a nurse is going against my wishes and continues to make inappropriate comments. *That's what I get for being responsible - that is the lesson I learned that day.*

Example 4: When I was eighteen, I thought joining the military was an excellent option. I'd have a place to stay, I would learn a skill, I would travel, and I could earn money. I met with my recruiter who drove me to where my very thorough military physical examination would take place.

I felt like I was doing pretty well until it was time for the pelvic exam. I was nervous, the doctor noticed and assumed that I was hiding something (pregnancy). I was not hiding anything.

He tried to reassure me that all the women have to come through his office and there is a nurse here to make sure there isn't any funny business going on. That didn't make me feel any better. I could feel myself getting emotional to which point I was asked if this was my first exam. I said it was not, but in full disclosure, I was sexually abused as a child, so these exams are not comfortable for me.

I assume the position on the table, feet in the stirrups, the nurse is standing to my right by feet, and there isn't a privacy sheet of any kind. The doctor proceeds with his index finger, using his other hand to push down on my abdomen which was not gentle, there were no warnings given. Just when I think it's over, two fingers and more pressure is applied. I'm a hot mess. I'm feeling violated, and there was a complete lack of being sensitive to my situation, and he was very rough, which I felt was unprofessional.

You get an eighteen-year-old young woman that comes forward as a rape victim; you are expected to handle things delicately, not cram your sausage fingers in with such force that you leave her tender area bruised. Then make her feel worse with your comments that you think she's mentally unstable.

I got to the very end of the physical examination process before finding out that the x-ray of my spine was 3 degrees more than the military was allowed to accept. *Well isn't that nice! If they had started with the x-ray, I could have saved their time and spared my dignity.*

Example 5: When I was eleven or twelve, I had gone to the dentist to get my first cavity filled. I wasn't a stranger to Novocain, in fact, I was a great patient for my primary dentist. The new dentist applies the numbing agent on my gums and injects the Novocain; he waits a few minutes to make sure it sets before he starts drilling. Sounds pretty typical, right?

I was in pain; this wasn't me being a baby or me being a brat. I was honestly in pain. My mouth was numb where the work was being done, but I felt him drilling. Once again, I am ignored. The dentist thought I was being difficult and proceeded to fill the cavity while I'm in tears. I have never feared my old dentist, but I felt this new guy was a hack. Just another professional with a poor bedside manner.

The reason for my pain would come to surface 20+ years later by a dentist who took a few moments to LISTEN to me and assess what was happening and questioned why several shots of Novocain wasn't effective.

The nerves in your mouth meet in the middle at the roof of your mouth. If you are having work done on the left side of your mouth, only the left side will get Novocain. The same applies to the right side of your mouth.

Unless you're like me and your nerves intersect and cross over at the middle of the roof of your mouth. If work is being done on my right side, the left side also needs to be numbed.

See I'm not crazy! I just need people to LISTEN and stop dismissing my concerns. I am not a classic textbook case; you may be required to think outside of the box if I'm your patient.

———————————

Example 6: There were a couple of times shortly after I left Max when he contacted me to meet up so we could talk. By "talk" he had made attempts to kiss me, grope me and want to know if I was up for having sex for "Old Times Sake." I turned down Max's advances, and I was forced to push him off of me. My no didn't mean no to Max. My no only made him want to try harder.

I can see how many couples who try to break off the relationship, fall back into the same habits. It's scary when you are feeling vulnerable and having to do things for yourself for the first time. There is a sense of comfort with your former partner, but you have to remember that you left for a reason. Your relationship wasn't healthy for either of you. Trust that in time, you will appreciate that you kept your distance.

———————————

Example 7: Since I was a young female in a mostly male-dominant workplace, I saw my fair share of gender inequality, sexual harassment and times when my no was falling on deaf ears.

During my earlier years, I was working part-time while in school at the dealership that my instructors had set me up filing repair orders for the Service Department. Most of the shuttle drivers were retirees, and there was one particular shuttle driver that targeted me.

I was seventeen, while "Bob" was easily in his fifties. "Bob" would often stand behind me and rub my shoulders and try to run his hands through my hair. He would hint that he could take care of me and I wouldn't have to work another day in my life. "Bob" wasn't taking my hints and asked me to dinner on a few occasions.

"Bob's" advances started off as an older guy being friendly, started to get very creepy and uncomfortable. I let my manager know how "Bob" was making me feel and I was assured that he would be talked too about his behavior. My manager made good on his word. I had noticed that my manager was keeping a close eye on "Bob" when I was around. "Bob" had been caught making advances towards me and my boss called him out in front of everyone within earshot. "Bob" was told to leave me alone, I just wanted to do my job and not be harassed by a man twice my age.

Example 8: Within that same year, I was also working weekends at another dealership that was part of the same company as the Chrysler/Jeep dealership. I worked as the weekend receptionist and dealt mostly with the salesmen.

I am now dealing with another much older greasy co-worker that also wants to be my sugar daddy. "Mark" had asked me to lunch on several occasions and thought by mentioning his expensive taste in food and wine that I would be impressed. I was feeling more nauseated than impressed.

Why is it so hard for men to not accept NO for an answer? These guys were certainly not god's gift to women, but they thought they were. Maybe they weren't used to hearing NO. Hooking up with older men was not at all appealing to me. I didn't want to be just another notch on their belt. Besides, they were co-workers, it was gross, and I made it a rule to never to date anybody I worked with. Work was work; it was how I made a living.

———————————

Example 9: While I was in Florida, I had two customers that couldn't take a hint either. Both "Doug" and "Miguel" knew I was in a relationship because they asked. But that didn't stop them from trying.
Some men took my pleasant nature and friendliness the wrong way. When you're working with the public, being friendly comes with the territory, it's part of providing excellent customer service. My friendliness was mistaken or confused with me showing "interest" that went beyond my duties.

"Doug" had befriended me and we hung out with mutual friends on a few occasions (which included my boyfriend at the time). So it's not like he had any chance with me. I wasn't interested in him in that way. I had gotten to know "Doug" over the course of six months, and I didn't feel awkward or threatened, maybe I was young and naive.

"Doug" invited me over to check out the work that he had done to his El Camino, as a friend, I agreed to stop by later. I checked out his car, and then he wanted to show me some of the decals and accessories that he wanted to put on, but they were in his house. I felt a little uneasy; I won't lie. But I had been able to trust "Doug" so far, so I made the exception since his mother was also home.

"Doug" showed me the accessories and seemed excited about getting his car fixed up. Then he leaned in to kiss me, and I had to put on the brakes. I let him know that I was just a friend, nothing more. He apologized for mistaking my friendship for something more. I don't recall seeing "Doug" after that.

As for "Miguel," he assumed the same thing "Doug" had about my friendly nature meaning more than what it was. I had suspected that "Miguel" had a crush on me and his frequent visits became a running joke among my co-workers. "Miguel" gained a bit of confidence during his frequent shopping and buying the least expensive items, so he could talk to me at my register.

"Miguel" would try to hold my hand when he was giving me his payment. He started complimenting me, how he thought I was beautiful as he tried to whisper in my ear. I realized I had a problem on my hands (literally), he didn't want to let go.

I let both of my managers know what he had been doing and how it had escalated. They agreed that I didn't have to run his transactions through anymore. I was allowed to walk away from my register and alert a manager if I notice him come in. My managers would take care of "Miguel" while I stayed out of sight until he left. That idea worked out for his next few visits, but sometimes I couldn't avoid him if I was the only cashier on and I had a lineup of customers.

"Miguel" took things too far one morning. It's possible he was staking out in the parking lot and waiting for me to arrive for my shift. He caught me by surprise when I was getting out from my vehicle. "Miguel" is trying to hold my hand and whisper in my ear asking why I won't give him a chance and how can he prove his love to me. He was trying to pull me to him and kiss me, but I kept resisting and pulling away. I now know how the cat in the Pepe le Pew cartoons must have felt. I found that I could not get away fast enough or far enough.

I had convinced him that I needed to get inside to start my shift. He made the connection that if I lost my job, he wouldn't be able to stop by and see me. Once again, my no didn't mean no, it obviously meant *KEEP TRYING; I'M PLAYING HARD TO GET!*

Once I got inside, and my managers saw who followed me in, they were quick to react. One manager walked with me to the back room while the other manager pulled "Miguel" aside and told him to stop harassing me. "Miguel" was told that his business was no longer welcome in that store and if he were seen walking in again, the police would be called. That was the last time I saw "Miguel."

How did I become this creepy older guy magnet? Was there a jumbo-sized blinking light above my head that read: "I'm secretly into older creepy guys, my no's mean yes"?

I'd like to say that those examples listed above were the only cases, but there are too many to list. Just know that they all begin with men mistaking my kindness while I'm doing my job as a means of "wanting more" from them.

I didn't want anything from these customers/co-workers that went beyond my duties for work. I wasn't the flirtatious type, my uniforms for work were black polyester pants with a colorful three button golf style shirt with the company logo accompanied with my name tag.

There are those who still think that what a woman wears is inviting unwanted behavior. I am not one of those believers. Women should be able to wear what they want to wear, and men should respect us enough to keep their filthy hands off of us. Don't get me wrong; I'm not just calling the men out. Some women have crossed the line with younger guys; which is also unacceptable.

———————————

My long-winded point is that many of us that work in customer service or the retail sector are going to smile at you, make small talk and laugh at your jokes. We are only doing our job, plain and simple, nothing more. If you make advances and get turned down, MOVE ON. Don't mistake our kindness or attention to detail as anything more than us providing excellent customer service.

I feel that it is important to mention and make very clear that just because you have a spouse doesn't mean they have automatic consent 24/7. You are not obligated to engage in any sexual activity against your will, no matter how long you've been married.

It's your body, you can say NO, and you don't need to have a reason. Saying No should be enough for the other person to back off. You are not a piece of property. If you couldn't say NO due to being drugged or on heavy medication or you were incapacitated in any way, then you could not have given your consent.

If you find that you are a target for unwanted attention at school, work, out in public, don't be afraid to ask for help. Until no means no to everyone, we are going to have to look out for one another.

I was lucky that I had a few managers that were willing to step up and do the right thing. I was grateful that my concerns were heard and taken seriously. If you have a co-worker that confides in you about being sexually harassed, please don't take it lightly or make jokes about their "boyfriend or girlfriend" at the workplace. You're only making matters worse. Choose to be part of the solution, not part of the problem.

I attribute all of these circumstances as my reasoning for rarely going out by myself. Not that my life is hindered in any way, but I believe in safety in numbers. I'm a short, petite framed woman and I know that physically I don't stand a chance against most men. I'd rather not put myself in a situation where I can be singled out.

I have learned to become hyper-aware of my surroundings, and I have developed a keen sense of direction. There is a part of me that is always in fight/flight mode when I'm out in public. I won't go to large outdoor venues or concerts alone. Maybe it's a form of PTSD that I have been able to deal with in my own way.

The thought of being kidnapped or getting lost in a crowd haunts me. I make it a point to know where the exits are and use word association to remember where I've parked my car while using parking garages or when the parking lot is huge. Maybe it's just a Hannah thing? I don't have a solid answer for this quirky behavior.

I will ask Jay to accompany me to all of my medical and dental appointments. His presence in the room brings me a sense of comfort. Jay understands my fear of being taken advantage of and that I often get emotional and frustrated when I feel that I am not being heard.

CHAPTER 9:

Recurring Dreams & My Forgiveness Technique

"Lessons in life will be repeated until they are learned." - Frank Sonnenberg

D reaming is normal for most of us; I say most of us because I do know a few people that claim they don't dream at all while they're sleeping. While many of my dreams appear to be random, vivid, bizarre or easily forgotten; I have others that make regular visits. It's hard to ignore the recurring nightmares that span over three decades. These recurring dreams are like trying to solve a puzzle with pieces that don't seem to fit or getting clues to a mystery, but the clues need to be decoded first. I know that there is a message or a lesson to be learned, but it's never direct; instead, they're always cryptic.

DREAM 1: ON THE RUN

Since my trauma thirty years ago; I have experienced several recurring dreams. The first of which the location never seemed familiar but I was always being chased. The person chasing me was never the same person; I didn't recognize them, nor was there something about them that seemed familiar. The premise was always the same. I would run, hide and tried calling for help. If I was able to find a phone; I knew the phone number but would always misdial over and over. I never made a successful phone call for help, and I would wake up just before getting caught.

This dream took place at least a few times a month for thirty years. Forever being chased by an unknown person, for reasons unknown. Unable to call for help and waking up just before getting caught or in some cases severely beaten or killed.

This sounds like I felt during my childhood. George was always seeking ways to do his dirty work. I would often hide or make myself scarce or hard to get when he was around. In some ways, my calls for help were never heard.

This could also fit my time with Max during the last couple of years of our relationship. I had been isolated and felt that I had no one to call for help, his mental games were exhausting. My life felt like a vicious circle with no means of escaping.

DREAM 2: LOST & FOUND

The next dream started after I left the Thompson's and continued to resurface at least once a month for thirty years. This dream always started off with me at the Thompson's house, just as I remember it. In many cases, I would be there visiting for a bit before making my way into the basement where my room used to be before I moved out. The bedroom was how I remembered it with posters on the wall with the furniture in place. I recall feeling rushed while sifting through my belongings that remained in there. Some items I recognized while others felt familiar, maybe because I've come across them in previous reenactments. The dream ends the same; with me looking through my old things feeling like there must be something I left behind but never end up leaving with anything.

A similar dream takes place at Mrs. Smith's house in my old bedroom. The same premise as the dream above and it started after I moved out of the house of chaos. I'm feeling rushed, searching through my belongings that seem familiar and recalling memories that are attached, but I leave never taking anything with me. I wake up before I can find whatever I'm looking for.

A similar dream takes place at the house with Max. This dream is slightly different, in the sense that I feel like I have to sneak into the house. Once I gain entry, I am walking through the house looking for my belongings and feeling like there is something important I need to retrieve. Max comes home, and I'm detected. He questions why I'm there, and the dream always ends with Max trying to get back together with me, and I turn him down. Max has made other appearances, but it's still the same scenario. Max won't take no for an answer, and I'm pushing him away from me.

In all of these dreams, the reality was that I was never completely ready to leave or I felt rushed to leave. At each home, I actually left many belongings behind. To dig a little deeper, I had left a part of myself behind in each location unintentionally. All of those nights I spent searching for that one object I was sure would stick out, that object never did appear.

At the Thompson's, I left the happy young thirteen-year-old version of myself behind.

At Mrs. Smith's, I left my childhood behind and was forced to become an adult and take care of myself. I left Hannah the firecracker behind. I also left Joey behind.

At my house with Max, I lost my best friend, I left his family that considered me an honorary member since I was thirteen years old. They were my family for almost 15 years. I spent more time with them than I had with my mother and brother. That was extremely hard to walk away from.

That's another breakthrough!

DREAM 3: THIRD WHEEL

Another one of my recurring dreams has two of my friends from sixth grade. In reality, we were very close that year in school, always hanging out together. Once junior high school started, we all had different classes, and we only saw each other at lunch. High School started two years later, and I didn't follow my friends to the public high school. Life continued to move on, and we never stayed in touch. In the dream, I'm spending time with one or the other, sometimes both of them. There is a part of me that is happy to spend time with them and try and catch up on what's been going on. But the other part of me can't help but feel like the loser friend that is desperate for their attention. I sense that they are only being polite, but they don't want to hang out with me. My feelings are hurt because I don't comprehend what went wrong with our friendship. In most cases, I would wake up feeling sad or rejected and wondering whatever happened to them.

This dream made sense to me after one of my therapy sessions. I had realized that while I was still interested in rekindling those friendships, those old friends had outgrown me. I decided to incorporate those two in my forgiveness session. It was not healthy for me to dwell on wanting to maintain a connection with two people that were no longer interested, for whatever reason.

DREAM 4: LOSING MY TEETH

These dreams have been happening for as long as I can remember. I always notice that one tooth is loose and for some reason, it doesn't stop with that one tooth. As I'm rinsing my mouth to get the blood out from the first missing tooth, more keep teeth coming out. The more I rinsed, the more teeth would fall into the sink.

I used to have this dream a couple of times a month, for years. I would associate it with the need to make an appointment with the dentist. Research provided many interpretations, such as:

Insecurities about personal loss, Anxiety about sexual experience, Life changes/growing pains, Fear of getting older, a desire to nurture yourself more carefully, signs of personal expansion, a chance to explore your feelings of loss and personal growth, making a costly compromise, the fear of being powerless or the idea of powerlessness as it pertains to your safety.

Well, all of those interpretations seem to fit at one point in my life. I had found that as this dream would come up, I was usually facing a hard decision or wondering which option was the better option.

It would be so much simpler if my dreams were more direct. Rather than confirming that I have an important choice to make, why not lead me to the best option? Showing me my teeth falling out doesn't comfort me at all. Wishful thinking, I suppose.

Enough was enough already! I was so tired of feeling like a prisoner in my mind. These cryptic nightmares had been replaying like a broken record in my head for a good part of my life.

I decided to try the same technique that I used six months ago to stop my high school bullies from living rent-free in my head. I figured that it was worth a try.

If you are at the stage where you are ready to evict your figurative freeloading tenants out for good, this technique can help you to achieve a sense of peace.

MY FORGIVENESS TECHNIQUE

First, I made a list as to who I wanted to forgive and what the action was that caused me to harbor ill feelings toward that person.

Second, I chose to sit in bed where I had the room to myself, and I read each grievance aloud; allowing a short pause in between to give myself a moment to feel any emotion attached.

As I read each grievance, I imagined that I was holding onto a balloon filled with helium. I continued by saying, "I forgive you because I deserve peace" and let go of that imaginary balloon and watched it float away.

I am happy to report that I have not had a single recurring dream in over two months since I completed my forgiveness session. Two months might not seem like a long enough time, but considering my recurring dreams were monthly, that's a significant improvement. I feel that I was somehow able to reclaim a small part of myself back.

The act of forgiveness is difficult. It's important to remember that the act of forgiveness doesn't mean that you agree with how another person treated you or that you find their behavior was acceptable. We forgive because we deserve peace, we deserve to move on and forward in our lives. Most importantly, don't forget to forgive YOURSELF.

It's time to ditch the freeloaders that have been holding you back.

By all means, feel free to modify this technique if there's another way that works better for you. I thought it was vital for me to share the method that works for me. It was not taught or anything that I researched. This technique was something I visualized at that moment, and it made sense to me.

I know, it sounds too easy, right? The ability to forgive is that simple; it's the internal struggle within ourselves and the misconception that the act of forgiving means you are accepting responsibility or admitting guilt. That is not true at all. You are letting go of the negativity that is attached, an energy that is not yours to carry.

These are a few inspirational quotes that helped me:

"Today I decided to forgive you. Not because you apologized, or because you acknowledged the pain that you caused me, but because my soul deserves peace." - Najwa Zebian

"Forgive yourself for not having the foresight to know what now seems so obvious in hindsight." - Judy Belmont

"Forgiveness is not about letting someone off the hook for their actions, but freeing ourselves of the negative energies that bind us to them." - Satsuki Shibuya

"Forgiveness is not an occasional act, it is a constant attitude." - Martin Luther King Jr

CHAPTER 10:

Breaking Free from my Mental Prison

"In life, you will realize there is a role for everyone you meet. Some will test you, some will use you, some will love you and some will teach you. But the ones who are truly important are the ones who bring out the best in you. They are the rare and amazing people who remind you why it's worth it" – *Unknown*

I am one of those people that has a hard time asking for help. I tend to be the suffer in silence type that will struggle through to prove to myself that I can do it. My husband reminds me often that it's okay to ask for help. This is one issue I've been working on over the last ten years. I have a hard time letting go of my independence.

Within the last year and a half, I've been able to reconnect with my cousin Victoria through Facebook. I had noticed that her posts had become cries for help. I had posted on my page that I am a safe person to come forward to and I was available to listen or talk should anyone need a shoulder to cry on or just an ear to listen.

Victoria felt that my post spoke directly to her, and she was compelled to come forward about how she was feeling and what had been on her mind. Victoria was dealing with a lot of stress, anxiety, depression and had felt that if she were to come forward to her immediate family, she might be rejected.

While Victoria's story is not mine to tell, I will say that she now had someone to confide in. Victoria and I were close as kids, literally. There are less than eight weeks that separate our birthdays. When we had a chance to play together, we were two peas in a pod, at least for the first nine years.

Over the last eighteen months, we've been able to pick up where we left off as if the thirty-year gap never happened. I've been able to help Victoria regain her self-confidence and provide a different perspective on what's troubling her. We appreciate each other's' honesty (while it's hard to hear) because it helps us to see the situation for what it is.

While I'm thinking I'm helping my cousin through her journey, Victoria has opened my eyes to who I used to be and how I used to handle things. I often get fired up over how Victoria is being mistreated and emotionally abused at home and while working. My empowering statements and encouraging comments for Victoria to stand up for herself has triggered a part of myself that had been dormant for over twenty years.

Hannah the firecracker had been awoken, and she wants to be tagged back in (wrestling reference) in true Ultimate Warrior style. Hannah the pistol, Hannah that doesn't take any shit had been well rested, and she's ready for action. Welcome back Hannah, you have been missed!

If you guessed that this moment was another breakthrough, you would be correct. Time to give quiet Hannah a rest, she's had a rough twenty plus years. Thank You, Victoria!

It wasn't long before I had come to terms with wanting to make changes in my life and wanted to seek professional help. It was time that I start taking my own advice.

I had reached a point where I was finally ready to get away from being a victim and become a survivor. I had made a list of mental blocks that I wanted help working through. I consulted my husband for his input as well. I wanted to make sure I wasn't in denial about anything. Jay thought this was a great idea and he was ready to support me in any way that he could.

I highly recommend that anyone who has endured a trauma that is similar to mine, please seek professional help and start your healing journey when you are ready. Forcing yourself to get help or being forced to attend therapy will not be as beneficial to you. You must be ready to move forward; only then will the healing process begin. If you are prepared, then your next step is to do a bit of research and find a certified professional that is trained to help you work through your trauma. Keep in mind that it took me 30 years to get to this point.

During my first session, I was encouraged to use the notebook provided to write down any thoughts or concerns that I had, and they would be discussed at the next session.

Once I started writing, it was hard to stop. The words kept coming, and the tears started flowing as this process seems to come naturally for me. Please keep in mind that each personal healing journey will vary in time. Some of us take longer than others; while sometimes we find a method that works and we run with it. Try not to compare your level of progress with the level of personal growth from another person, as each case is different.

During my second session, there was quite a bit to discuss. The common theme of my scattered thoughts was a scared little girl whose voice was not heard desperately wanted to be acknowledged. Not like in a multiple personality disorder way, but rather as my inner child or that part of myself that was holding me back in some manner. I hope that makes sense, as I don't know how else to describe it.

It was suggested that I tap into that part of me, my inner child that was scared, she wanted answers, she wanted to be heard and try to find out why she hasn't let go. To console that part of me so that I could put that part of me to rest; I decided to write a heartfelt letter to my nine-year-old self to let her know that I understand, I get it and reassuring her that we are safe now.
Seems that in some way she was not aware that thirty years had passed and we had grown up. My letter to my inner child

ended up being thirteen pages long. It ends with me offering a hug and one last good cry together before I take over with a promise not to screw it up.

In some way, knowing that part of me exists helps to keep me accountable for my choices going forward. Almost as if I'm the parent looking out for a child that had been through an awful lot and was not equipped to process what was going on.

During my last session, we discussed my recurring dreams as that was one mental block that I was not able to work out on my own. These are the same dreams that were mentioned in the last chapter. I was able to write in my journal and work through them while having a breakthrough moment about my grandfather David.

It was that moment that I had put the pieces together about Grandfather David and was trying to cry quietly as not disturb my husband as he had just got settled in bed. My sniffling was detected, and that prompted an emotional conversation that went well past 4:00 am.

Jay wanted to talk through my emotions and see why I was so upset and what triggered that response. As I had mentioned in a previous chapter, I was deeply hurt when I realized that I cared for a family member and tried so hard to gain his acceptance, only to realize that I was just a passing thought to him.

Our conversation continues, and Jay is trying to understand what it must have been like for me. He doesn't have the experience to pull from, but he still gets a gold star for his effort and trying to put himself in my shoes. Jay feels there must have been a divine strength that stepped in to watch over me because he couldn't believe that I had never resorted to drugs or alcohol as a means of escaping my situation.

Jay had asked me why I didn't take those routes, what was keeping me so strong? At first, I didn't know but then a moment later it dawned on me. I did for Joey. What an eye-opener! I couldn't believe that I had never made that connection. I didn't realize that I had taken on the protective role maybe even a parental role for Joey.

My mother had said something to me years ago that resonated with me. She told me that the day would come when Joey and I would be all that we had. Since I was the oldest, I needed to promise her that I would watch out for Joey. I assumed she was talking about after she passes away it would just be the two of us. I don't think she expected that I would have to fill that role as soon as I did.

If I lost myself to drugs or drinking, then that would have left Joey alone, he would have nobody in his corner. It was important for me to be that one family member that didn't turn their back and run when things got tough. I wanted him to grow up to know that he had one person that cared about him. His victories were my victories. I couldn't just leave him as our parents had left us.

That epiphany prompted me to write Joey a letter. I felt that he should know that he played an essential role in my life and I wanted to thank him. Had it not been for the fact that I had a little brother to watch out for; I don't know what would've happened to me. That letter ended up being six pages long. It was that emotional letter that sparked the idea for this book.

I had mentioned during one of my therapy sessions that I had bought two books that I thought might help me on my healing journey.

It Didn't Start With You: How Inherited Family Trauma Shapes Who We Are & How To End The Cycle - Mark Wolynn

This book spoke to me as I wanted to find out which issues I needed to claim ownership of, and which aspects were not mine to carry. I do recommend this book if your family also has a history of trauma. While I don't want to spoil the book for you, I will mention a few examples that fit my situation.

The author suggests that when your mother is still a fetus, she can inherit any residual stress or trauma that her mother is experiencing during the pregnancy. While your mother is still a fetus, she will have all of the eggs that she will be born with, before you come into the world. Are you with me so far?

If your grandmother or mother experience trauma or a complicated pregnancy before you are born, it is possible that you may experience residual effects that were passed down through DNA. In my case, my mother suffered a loss of a child, she had been abused as a child, and she had a stressful pregnancy while carrying me, thanks to my alcoholic father.

It is possible that some of my issues or fears are not mine at all. Not that I'm passing the blame, but it makes sense in my case that I could be reacting to phantom stress or fears that belong to my grandmother, or more likely my mother. Just as the residual effects could come from your father, uncle or aunt and they could skip over you and attach to the next sibling in line.

This book does give plenty of examples from real patients as well as many exercises that you can work through to help you figure out what may have been passed down to you and by whom if you feel inclined to dig a little deeper.
As I sit here writing and looking back on my past, I have to consider that maybe one choice that I made for myself, wasn't really for me. I may have unknowingly made a choice to please my parents as a way to make them proud.
My father was disappointed that I wasn't a boy. My mother had enrolled in the automotive program in high school. My mother was teased and harassed so much that she dropped out in her junior year. Both stories I had heard years before making my choice to enter the automotive program.

While I did find it interesting and I am proud to have finished the program; I was never passionate about it. Not like my peers who were going to car shows and swap meets or restoring old classics.

Was it possible that I was so determined to prove that I could take an interest in a male dominant hobby to gain the acceptance from my absent father?

Did I feel sorry that my mother wasn't able to fulfill her interest during high school that I provided the opportunity for her to live vicariously through me?

Had my choice been an attempt to fill a void where a father teaches his daughter?

Had my choice been just a coincidence?

In any case, I do believe things happen for a reason, whether we are aware of the purpose at that moment or not. I don't regret my choice, but for now, that answer lies in limbo.

The Sexual Healing Journey: A Guide for Survivors of Sexual Abuse - Wendy Maltz

This book comes highly recommended by many survivors and therapists. I have not come to a point where I'm ready to start the sexual healing while the personal healing is still a work in progress. One thing at a time; I don't want to feel overwhelmed or rushed in my healing process.
I am confident that this book will help me to accomplish the goals that I wish to achieve in the very near future.

There a few things that I have trouble overcoming in the bedroom. I am hesitant to initiate intimacy because there is a part of me that doesn't want to push that act on my partner. I know what it feels like and I don't be the one to cause those feelings for anyone else to experience. Maybe there is a fear of being rejected. It would be my luck that the one time I have to courage to initiate intimacy, I get turned away.

There is a part of me that feels ashamed almost like it's forbidden for me to want to engage in sexual activity. I don't know if that comes from the double standard that females face. It's normal for guys to have sex but girls are considered or labeled as sluts.

I have an issue with nudity, in general. I am uncomfortable in my own skin. I don't feel attractive, gorgeous or sexy and I expect that my partner sees the same thing I do. I am uncomfortable around people that wear too little clothing or show too much of themselves. I am not comfortable looking at my partner in the nude. There is a part of me that feels I shouldn't look, it's wrong to look and I will overt my eyes because I don't want them to feel as uncomfortable as I feel in that moment. Beaches and water parks do not make the list of my favorite places to have fun and relax.

This lack of comfort even affects movies, and TV shows that I watch with scenes of nudity or if there is a sex scene. I feel ashamed to be watching like a teenager trying not to get caught watching porn. I reach for the remote to turn down the volume. It's silly I know. I can't help but feel that if my partner walks in and catches the scene that he will be turned on enough to want to have sex and I don't want to turn him down. Then again, I grew up with sex being taboo; it was for procreation, not recreation. Movies like Magic Mike or Fifty Shades of Grey would make me very uncomfortable to sit through.

Sex is never the first thing on my mind, or the second, or the third. In fact, sex ranks so low that I have been satisfied with participating just once a month. I have given so little thought to the idea of pleasuring myself, that I don't participate in any form of self-exploration.

I do want to have a healthier, normal sex life with my husband. I want to be able to participate in regular husband/wife cuddling and being playful without my mind quickly putting up protective walls because those actions "could' lead to sex.

Once I'm in the zone, I'm ok-ish. My mind wanders, and I tell myself to relax and allow myself to enjoy it. I do climax and feel satisfied, and I'm quick to cover up or get dressed. I'm not comfortable just being naked, except for showering.

Maybe it's my way of controlling the situation because there have been many times in my past where sex was forced, or I felt obligated and never saw the benefit for me. A former partner got what he wanted, and I was done when he was done. More often than not, I was left feeling used because there was a lack of emotion or passion. Very self-serving, only his needs were met.

I can do better. I want to be better, and Jay deserves better. He's been so very patient with me. While my inadequacies aren't posing any immediate threats on our marriage, I don't want them to get out of control to where Jay loses interest in me altogether.

One more issue for me to work through is the fact that I am unable to get a full night's rest. My usual sleep routine starts with my mind wandering before settling down. I sleep the best during the first two to three hours; I can usually sleep through anything. Once the fourth hour arrives, I am constantly tossing and turning.

It feels like every 30-45 minutes I'm waking up to adjust my position and need a few minutes to fall back to sleep before it all over again during the next three or four hours of light sleeper mode. Or as Jay calls it, High Alert mode.

One theory is that due to the frequency that I was woken up in the middle of the night as a kid either by my mother or by George makes sense. My body may have learned to adjust that behavior as the new normal. Maybe it's the inner little girl that still feels that she is not safe at night. This sleep pattern has been going on for as long as I can remember.

I know there were many nights that I felt like I had to be on High Alert with George around. He was known to snatch me up while I was asleep and I recall many sleepless nights thanks to him.

Another theory could be since my back/spine aren't getting any younger, that I may need a softer mattress topper. Or maybe since I've gained a bit of weight in the midsection, that I need to lose weight; which I am in the slow but steady process of doing. I have noticed when we travel that if the mattress is softer, I sleep better or at least more comfortable.

Jay is convinced that we need a few nights without our two pugs sharing the bed. I have spent many nights in bed by myself, no pugs because they stay in the living room while Jay was on an overnight schedule. I'm still unable to get a restful night's sleep.

I do have one memory when I was younger, maybe five years old. It was like a scene from a Disney animated movie. I remember waking up, and the sun was shining through the window. I hopped out of bed, looked out the window and thought to myself, what a beautiful morning it was. The birds were chirping with a light breeze coming in from outside, and it was peaceful.

That was the one, and only time I recall waking up and feeling fully rested. This was just before George had entered my life and all of the uprooting began.

My internal clock won't allow me to sleep in beyond 7:00-7:30 am. I was awake for school for twelve years, then needed to be awake for work by that time; which lasted for fifteen years. It's to a point where I rarely need to rely on an alarm clock to ensure I am awake on time. In most cases, I'm up a few minutes before it is set to go off. Creature of habit, I guess. Even at a semi-retired lifestyle, with no reason to be up that early, but like clockwork, I'm awake when the sun comes up.

What I really need is a zero-gravity bed in a sensory deprivation room.

I have avoided making regular doctor and dentist appointments for routine physicals and check-ups unless I needed to be seen to clear an infection that over the counter medicine couldn't handle.

This behavior continues because I have lost confidence due to interactions with previous medical professionals. I was tired of going to them for advice on a personal matter, only to leave feeling violated, insulted and ignored.

I know that getting routine physicals and check-ups are essential, especially since I'm coming up on my 40th milestone and early menopause is just around the corner. It's difficult to shake the feeling of shame when it comes to making an appointment for the pelvic/Pap test. I reluctantly make the appointment, and I'm a bundle of stress and anxiety while I'm waiting for examination to be over. While the exam is taking place, I always get emotional and start crying. Not in an inconsolable sort of way, but involuntarily.

I can't help it, the feelings from previous events remind me of how violated I was. Assuming the position on the table is a reminder of encounters I'd like to forget. *Even writing this causes an emotional reaction.*

I've got to the point where I feel that I have to let the nurse/doctor know that there is a good chance that I will get emotional and assure them that it's not them, it's me. Some have shown compassion as they have seen this before in other patients, which helps a bit.

I've had the same doctor for the last eight years, I've only seen him twice. Once for a TB skin test for entry into college which also included an MMR booster and the second visit was for my consultation for a tubal ligation procedure.

When I was looking for a new doctor, the application had asked if I had a preference as to male or female. Yes, I do have a preference, and I stated that I would prefer a woman. As I go back to the clinic to hand in the paperwork as a new patient; I mentioned to the receptionist/medical assistant that I really would prefer a female doctor. I was told that I would get paired up with whoever is in the rotation when my application is processed. *Then why bother giving your patient a choice?*

I was paired up with a male doctor, which I'm sure he's more than capable. Honestly from the two visits that I had with him, he appeared distracted by his electronic device, and I felt like a number. There wasn't a personal connection made, but rather a yeah, yeah let's get you in and out, I'm too busy to discuss your matters or answer your questions, NEXT!

I had decided to seek a female doctor in an attempt to work through my mental block in this area. In full disclosure, I will be meeting with her tomorrow as part of the Meet & Greet first visit as a new patient. I feel that I would be more apt to go more frequently if I had a doctor that I felt comfortable with and was able to build a sense of trust concerning my hesitations. It's a start in the right direction.

As you can see, I have made some progress on my own and through sharing my experience with all of you in this book. However, my journey is still ongoing.

As this book draws to a close I want to leave you with a final message:

From one survivor to another, you are not alone.

Don't be afraid to speak up and share your story, even if your voice trembles. I know that you didn't ask for this to happen, and it definitely is NOT your fault. No matter what others may have said to you. You are not confused or crazy, deep down you know that to be true.

It wasn't your clothes; it wasn't because you decided to go out with your friends to blow off steam. What you endured was not done out of love. A person that truly loves you and respects would never treat you that way. None of us ever "Asks For It."

You may be feeling ashamed, embarrassed, violated, maybe a loss of self-confidence, loss of self-worth or angry. Your feelings are valid and rational. It's okay to cry or scream because there is no shame in working through whatever emotions you are experiencing.
The actions against you have nothing to do with you, but everything to do with the sickness of your abuser. I know that things may not be all sunshine and rainbows today, but your life can get better. I don't expect you to forget what happened or how you feel, but I can assure you that in time the details will get blurry, and eventually they will start to fade away.

I hope that you decide to seek help when you are ready to heal from the emotional trauma that has surfaced. You deserve peace, and you deserve to feel safe. You shouldn't have to live in fear or have to look over your shoulder and sleep with one eye open. Asking for help is not a sign of weakness, none of us can do it alone. Consider joining a support group or group therapy if you feel that your family can't or won't help you.

If you are not ready to talk and start your healing journey, perhaps a creative outlet is better for you. Start painting, drawing, playing music, or writing in a journal. If you are more athletic or outdoorsy, try running, kickboxing, swimming, kayaking. Everyone needs an outlet to vent to get the anger and frustration out in a healthy manner. I encourage you to find one that works best for you.

Keeping things bottled up will only create more problems for you and your health. You do not have to go through your healing journey alone. You are loved. You are one of a kind. Your life matters. You have a voice that needs to be heard. You deserve closure. You deserve justice. You didn't choose to be a victim, but you can choose to be a survivor!

"Never stay silent so that someone else can stay comfortable" - Unknown

SUPPLIMENTAL:

Letter to my Inner Child

To My 9-year-old self,

I understand your pain; I understand your fears and hesitations.

You've had to grow up faster than you should have. You didn't have a role model, and you feel that those who were supposed to protect you, failed you.

Your father left when you were two years old. He never showed any interest in getting to know you. Your mother took the easy way out; she gave up her parental rights when you were 13. How could you not feel abandoned?

You've felt like your voice hasn't been heard and your concerns/fears have not been taken seriously. Even medical professionals have made you feel unheard and violated which has caused you to lose faith in their opinions.

I understand why you have trust issues. Some of your previous appointments were undoubtedly less than professional. You were rushed out and felt that you had been taken advantage of, yet again. Your hesitation to make regular appointments is not the best answer. That is all going to change. We finally have a female doctor that understands our concerns. We will no longer tolerate rude, insensitive medical/dental professionals. There are many professionals with a proper bedside manner that genuinely want to help us. We will make an effort to seek them out.

Knowing full well of the trauma you had endured, I understand your lack of trust and why you are not comfortable with your body. I understand why you are uncomfortable with nudity, initiating intimacy and your lack of a sex drive. You don't feel attractive and think others see your flaws; they can't possibly find you attractive. I also know that we are our own worse critics and hold our self to a higher standard.

You've found it hard to love yourself when you've felt unloved and disposed of by your parents, your grandmother and your first husband, Max.

You're restless at night and unable to get a good night's sleep. You are on high alert and in constant protective mode. Of course, you want to protect yourself. I remember those nights being woken up and carried out against your will.

I know that you have questions that you may never get an answer for. We have to stop dwelling on the "what if's" and embrace what we have today.

I want to acknowledge your contributions in keeping us safe and protecting us for the last 30 years. Thank You!

I want to help you, protect you, keep you safe and take over this burden that you've felt you've had to carry for so long. You should not have had to endure all that you did and maintain being strong for as long as you had.

I hear you. You have a voice, and I am listening.

Things have changed over the last 30 years, and you no longer need to be afraid, scared, or protective.

The man that violated you, he's been dead for over 20 years. You don't have to worry about him.

Your mother, we've had our ups/downs, but we are in control. There is nothing that she can say or do to hurt us on an emotional level. Our mother is not a threat to us in any way, and we have no issue cutting her out of our life if she crosses that line.

Your grandmother, the puppet master, has not been an issue for us since the early 2000's. We cut our ties with her back then and had never looked back. She doesn't pull on our strings, nor does have any control over us in any way.

Your father, we have allowed his absence to hurt us for years. So many questions will go unanswered. We did learn that he had his demons and struggled with alcoholism and PTSD. We have made peace with him, and we even have an open line of communication with our older half-sister. She's been an excellent resource for filling in some of the blanks.

Our first husband, we ignored the signs early on because we thought Max was the "one." His family loved us, as chaotic as they were, we felt like we belonged. Once the marriage could not be salvaged, we gathered our courage and left. We endured enough abuse and had decided No More! Max wanted us to look more like his childhood crush. We deserved better than that, and we deserved better than Max. Max is no longer our problem.

We are in the best position in our life right now. We have Jay who loves us for who we are. He embraces our flaws and doesn't want to change them. Jay looks out for us to make sure that we don't get taken advantage of. Jay knows that we are kind-hearted and some people have taken advantage of our kindness in the past.

Jay encourages us to follow our dreams, to pursue hobbies and doesn't make us feel that our interests are silly or stupid. Jay is very supportive. We attended college as an adult, we have shifted careers, we have pursued artistic hobbies, we are semi-retired and work from home. All because Jay believes in us and has encouraged us to do so.

Jay knows that we have been let down and we have lacked the proper support emotionally and financially. He's happy to be our pillar of strength, our shoulder to cry on and he's kept every promise he's ever made to us. Jay continues to be patient and understanding of the baggage that we brought into this marriage ten years ago. He wants us to be physically/emotionally healthy because there is no logical reason why we shouldn't be.

We don't have any threats or dangers. We have a wonderful husband and two pugs that love us. We are the happiest that we've ever been. What more could we ask for?

All of the things you have been worrying about and protecting us from; they are no longer a threat to us. Going forward, starting today, let me take on any burdens. Let me be the one to protect you and look out for you.

We have a family that loves us. We have a family that wants us and helped us move from the USA to Canada to be here. That has to hold some weight, right?

We are safe.
We are loved and wanted.
We don't have any threats.
We want to learn our karmic lesson so that we have a better life the next time around.

If the cycle of abuse is to stop with us, then I need your help to ensure that we don't pass our shortcomings on to our next life (lives).

I offer a genuine heartfelt hug and if we need one last good cry to get things out of our system; I'm okay with that too.

I'll take over from here. You can sit back and enjoy the next 30+ years. I promise not to screw it up.

Epilogue:
What Ever Happened To…

While I may never get closure with some things in my life; I wanted to be able to offer closure to you.

Brian: My father continued to call my mother until I was about 11 or 12-years-old. According to my mother, he would ask about me but never ask to speak to me. She suggested that he didn't want me to get my hopes up and get too attached.

Brian had agreed to write to me when I was eleven, so naturally, I took that opportunity. I wrote my first letter and filled him in on what had been going on in my life. At this point, I was living with the Thompson's and telling him about school and how happy I was to hear that he was interested in getting to know me.

I was eager to get a reply in the mail and was confident that it would come any day now. His letter never came. A couple of months had passed, and my mother had confirmed that Brian did get my letter and that I should not expect one from him. I was disappointed and thought he should know. I had sent a second letter explaining how I felt and not to worry; I would not contact him ever again. I had peace of mind knowing that I at least made an effort. Once he found out I was a ward of the state, he stopped calling my mother.

A few years had passed, at this point, I was living in the house of chaos. I had received a social security check in the mail. There was nothing inside to indicate why I was receiving this, only that I could expect to receive a check every month until I turned eighteen.

I was confused and wanted to make sure that I wasn't receiving this by mistake. I called the social security office to find out why. The agent had confirmed that it was not a mistake and that I should expect six more checks. When I asked why I was receiving them, I was not answered. The agent said that she was not at liberty to tell me why. I wanted to make sure I was reading between the lines. The agent did confirm that she did know but couldn't say. I thanked her for being so helpful.

It wasn't until seven years later when I was doing a bit of online research to put together my family tree when I found out that my father had died. I double checked the information, the birthday was correct, the name was correct, the location was right, and the date of death matched when I started getting those social security checks. I was disappointed to have found out in that manner, while also wondering why no one bothered to contact me directly. Someone must have known Brian had a younger daughter, and somebody must have known to the have those benefits sent to me.

Janet: My older half-sister from my father's first marriage. My mother had been honest with me, so I knew about Janet. I had wanted to reach out to Janet to find out about our father's medical history. I knew that alcohol played a significant role on that side of the family, but I wanted to know why our father died so young. Brian was a few months shy of his 50th birthday when he passed; actually, many of my relatives on that side all died before they reached 60 years old; naturally, I was concerned about my health.

I found Janet on Facebook, and I could tell right away it was her. I had never met her, but she looked like our father from the few pictures that I did see growing up. I sent her a message with details to prove that I was family, information that only she would know. Janet did reply and was surprised to find out that she had a younger half-sister. She remembers baby Cassandra and how her passing upset our father, but she didn't know he had remarried and had another daughter.

Somehow, I had managed to become the black sheep of the family. Brian's mother knew of me. In fact, she didn't even want to see me until I was at least five months old. Her reason was that she would be able to tell if I looked like my father or not at that age. She had agreed that I did look like him in front of my mother, but then told my father I look nothing like him after my mother left the room.

Janet spent a lot of time at her grandmother's house when she was younger, and Brian's mother never mentioned me to Janet. Janet had also spent a few days with our father just before he passed and he never said anything about me to her. It was all making sense as to why nobody contacted me about my father's death. He kept me a secret. Just more questions that I'll never get answered.

The door of communication is open between us. She had confirmed that our father passed away from prostate cancer. Janet had filled in some of our family's history and shared a few pictures that she has of our dad in Vietnam. She's happily married and living on the west coast with her high school sweetheart.

Max: My first husband and former best friend since junior high school. After our divorce, Max married Penny. From what I've been told and the pictures that had been shared on social media, their wedding was also the same day as a huge blizzard. I will admit to having a good laugh because their guests were miserable and I thought Karma had paid them a visit on my behalf.

Max had contacted me a few years later because he missed not having me to talk to when he needed a listening ear. He went on to tell me that Penny was treating him poorly, and a lot of what he was saying sounded very familiar. Penny was treating Max in the same manner that Max had treated me.

Karma strikes again! Max admitted that he had been seeing Mr. Peterson (therapist) for a while and it was suggested that Max should cease all forms of contact with me, he needed to move on. I agreed and wished him well going forward. I decided it was best to block Max from seeing my Facebook page and I changed my email address and blocked his number from my cell phone in case he felt tempted to contact me after that conversation. If Max needs to cut me out of his life, I'm all too happy to help.

From what I do hear and see, Max doesn't talk to his family as often as he used to. It seems his family is not a huge fan of Penny and Penny doesn't mind the wedge she's placed in the middle. *Not my circus, not my monkeys.*

Lou: Max's best friend since high school. Not much has changed in the lives of Lou, Tina, and Lexi. The only real piece of news worth sharing is that I was named Lexi's godmother just after Lexi was born. I had spent a lot of time with Lexi during her first three or four years. Max and I were at their house most weekends. The guys played hockey on the PlayStation and drank beer, and I'd play with Lexi while Tina was at work or if she had gone to bed.

About a year after I had moved up to Canada I get a message from Lou. He goes on to tell me that it's a real shame that I moved so far away. Lou said that my decision to move was a disappointment to him. He had expected that I would have taken my role of godmother seriously and he felt it was best to strip me of that honor and give it to Tina's sister (Max's dream girl) because she wasn't going to up and leave as I did.

I was furious! Eight years have passed, and I'm still shaking my head. Yes, I did move across the country, I did not just up and leave without saying goodbye or leaving no means of contacting me. I had remarried and started my life with a Canadian, one of us had to move. My family ties were not as strong as Jay's were to his family. It made sense that I'd be the one to move. *So sorry if my happiness disappoints you, Lou!*

I had been sending Lexi Christmas gifts every year, and I continue to send a little something to her. Lou is close to his godmother and wanted the same thing for Lexi. I understand that, but it's not like I was never going to come back and visit. I've made several trips back home and only once did he offer to bring Lexi to see me.

What's ironic is that Lexi and Joey's daughter are best friends, so Lexi is often over at Joey's house. Joey's family has become a second family to Lexi, and they invite her over and include her in their family outings. Joey took over where I left off.

Lou can strip me of that title all he wants. It doesn't change the fact that I still love Lexi and I'd move mountains for her.

Gina: Grandma Gina ended up getting a divorce from David. David passed away almost two years ago. My Uncle David is getting married soon. As I mentioned earlier, it would be fourteen years before I saw Grandma Gina again.

After fourteen years of having zero contact with my grandmother, the first thing she tells me is that a particular family member can't have kids due to low sperm count.

Not, Hi Hannah, how have you been? It's nice to see you!

Anyway, Grandma Gina is now dealing with dementia which runs strong on that side of the family. Since she is unable to care for herself, she's moved in with my mother. While that wasn't Gina's preferred option, my mother was the only one of her kids to step up and offer to help her.

Jon: My mother's boyfriend from high school, the one that got away thanks to Grandma Gina meddling and threatening.

Jon had moved on with his life and went on to marry Mila. There were many similarities between Mila and Marie. If Jon couldn't be with Marie, in his mind, Mila was a very close second. Jon and Mila had three kids of their own.

I don't recall how Jon and Marie reconnected over two decades ago, but I do remember spending time at their house and playing with Jon's kids and learning to play Uno at their kitchen table. I remember thinking that Jon was a nice guy, at least he was kind to me when I was 7 or 8 years old.

Once I started working in the automotive retail sector, I saw a lot more of Jon. He had become one of my frequent customers. He would come in to visit with me and ask about my mom. I was starting to get to know Jon and realized that he really cares for my mother and he'd even ask about Joey.

Jon had told me that he almost married my mother years ago, but my grandmother had prevented that from happening. Jon also mentioned that he thought of Joey and I as if we were his kids and would've loved to have been a father to us.

He had talked to me about Mila, told me that he loved her and his kids very much. Jon confessed that his heart always belonged to my mother.

Naturally, this conversation prompted me to call my mother and find out what happened.

Victoria: My cousin that had reached out to me during her time of crisis. I have since spoken to Victoria, and she gave me her blessing to share her story with you. Victoria had been struggling her whole life but could never put her finger on what the issue was. It might make more sense if I told you that she was born as a male. I grew up with my male cousin, Patrick.

Victoria knew as a child that she wasn't like the other boys, but in the early 1980's it was hard enough to come out as being gay. The term transgender was not as popular as it is today. Thirty years would pass before Victoria realized that she is transgender. By this time, she was a husband of 20 years and a father of two older teenagers. Victoria felt that she was a woman trapped in a man's body.

Over the last eighteen months, I've been helping my cousin through the transition process. Victoria has started her second level of hormone replacement therapy and has already noticed drastic changes to her body. I wish that I could say that her wife and kids support her choice, but they don't share my enthusiasm. They keep demanding she present herself as male while out in public with them. They were happy to buy clothes and makeup and attend the Pride Parade when they thought it was just a phase.

In one breath they will assure you that they don't have a problem with anyone in the LGBTQ community; while in the next breath my cousin is being told she is going to hell for being selfish, destroying their family and only thinking of her own happiness. They were happier when she was he/him/Dad/Husband.

The girls don't recognize that they still have both parents under the same roof. Regardless of what their transgender parent looks like on the outside, the love she has for her kids doesn't change.

How dare she stop living a lie and being deeply depressed? Can't she see that her happiness makes them uncomfortable? Is my sarcasm coming through?
But in all seriousness, I recognize how difficult their situation is, and I hope they can find a solution that works for everyone, not just a one-sided solution.

Joey: My little brother, Joey graduated high school and went on to enroll with the US Coast Guard; he was stationed in Alaska. Joey is now married to his lovely wife, Sara. Together they have three great kids. Joey plays an active role in the lives of his children. I'm very proud of the man that he has become.

Joey's love of animals has been passed on to his kids. They have a grumble of (four) pugs, two sphynx (hairless) cats, two lizards, and their three guinea pigs have found a new home with our cousin Victoria.

Marie: My mother ended up leaving Gerald thanks to the advice that I gave her. She realized that she wasn't happy, she was being used, emotionally abused and wanted to file for a divorce from husband number three.
I had talked to her about Jon and passed along his contact information, so she now had the option to get in touch with

him. My mother filled me in on the story and what happened when Jon asked Gina for her blessing. Jon had a chance to tell Marie about fifteen years earlier about what had taken place.

My mother decided to reconnect with Jon. Marie was on her way out of her marriage, and Jon was grieving the tragic loss of his wife, Mila. Marie and Jon had reentered each other's lives during a time when they both needed the support from an old friend.

Long story short. Marie and Jon did get married. Sure, it was in their sixties, but better late than never. It was during this short period when the family relationships were mended. Marie and her siblings were talking, and Joey had decided to give our mother a chance. Marie met her grandchildren for the first time at her wedding. Things had looked promising, but that was short lived.

Marie is currently taking care of her elderly mother with dementia; she's also taking care of Jon, who she has to stay on top of to ensure his insulin levels remain in check. Marie still doesn't talk to her siblings because they have cut ties with her. Marie's relationship with her mother is a daily challenge. Gina is still pulling the strings, and Marie continues to seek her mother's approval.

Jon is a saint for putting up with Gina. *It feels like there should be a lesson about not burning bridges in there somewhere.*

A few years ago, Joey had come to terms with allowing our mother back into his life. He was only ready for baby steps, taking things slow and easing back into it. Our mother was prepared for full steam ahead and felt that she had been waiting long enough.

Our mother isn't satisfied with being able to stay in touch through social media and seeing pictures of her grandchildren. Her private messages to both Joey and his wife had become a nuisance. I had to remind her that Joey, Sara, and their three kids are very busy with working full time and working on their college degrees, the kids are in school with their extra activities that keep them busy. It's almost like a part of her forgot what it was like to be a parent. She didn't have half of the responsibilities that Joey has with his family.

Our mother just doesn't get it, there is no connection that Joey is still very hurt, nor does she understand that the idea of her pop in visits caused Joey to experience a panic attack. I had tried telling our mother to back off and let her know it's not okay to drop by unannounced, but my advice has fallen on deaf ears. Our mother quickly wore out her welcome, and she doesn't realize just how close she is to losing all contact with Joey and her grandchildren.

There is a part of me that feels sad for her, while another part feels that she's done this to herself. She needs to acknowledge that her actions have consequences. Her choices caused her to lose her kids just as her choices caused her kids to suffer emotional wounds that may never fully heal.

This brings us around full circle. Thank You, for taking the time to read my story and allowing me the opportunity to be heard. At the very least you have a better understanding as to what life is like for an adult survivor of childhood sexual abuse. I hope that other survivors realize that they are not alone and gain the courage to break their silence and seek justice.

I'll leave you with one final quote:

"One small crack does not mean that you are broken. It means that you were put to the test and you didn't fall apart." - Linda Poindexter

WARNING:

Listen Up Parents

If you have continued reading up to this point, and my story has pulled at your heartstrings, or you found yourself cursing and shaking your head in disbelief over my mother's behavior then LISTEN UP!

I'm going to share with you some of the signs and behaviors a child might display if they have been sexually abused. Just a reminder folks, sexual abuse knows no gender, age, race or religion. In most cases, the abuser **IS** someone the victim knows, and the abuser isn't always male.

In no particular order:

- A child has a new toy/gift/ money given without reason. Many abusers will use gifts to bribe the victim into staying silent or as a means of trying to establish trust. In some cases, the gift may not be age appropriate, like an expensive necklace given to an 11-year-old girl.
- Refuses to talk about a secret shared with an older child or an adult.
- Plays, writes, draws or has dreams that depict or reference sexual interaction
- They might think their body is repulsive, bad or dirty
- The child may exhibit adult-like sexual behavior or language
- Has unexplained nightmares or other sleep issues like bed wetting if they are out of that phase.
- The child may resist removing clothing during baths, with their peers during gym class or changing for bed
- They may develop a new fear of certain places or people
- A sudden change in behavior, fear, rage, insecurity, withdrawal or have frequent mood swings
- The child might use new names for body parts
- Self-inflicted injuries, cutting, burning

- Substance abuse
- Display a fear of intimacy or closeness, maybe with a family member that they were once comfortable to be around.
- A sudden change in appetite, overeating, loss of appetite or trouble swallowing.
- They might leave "clues" to encourage you to discuss sexual issues
- Pain, discoloration, bleeding or discharge at the genitals, anus or mouth
- Pain while urinating or during a bowel movement
- A child might try to avoid family members, attending certain classes or avoid certain kids at school or on the bus.
- Unexplained pregnancy

As for myself, I displayed/experienced eight of these signs that went unnoticed as a child. Now as an adult I am still working through two of these behaviors.

Should your child or any child for that matter come forward to you about being abused, take it VERY seriously. Do not dismiss their concerns. It takes a great deal of courage to come forward especially if they have been threatened not to say anything.

Try to stay calm if you happen to have this conversation. Take the child aside and continue listening where you can have a bit of privacy. Take the child to a hospital to allow them to run the proper tests including tests for HIV and Sexually Transmitted Diseases and to collect evidence while also treating signs of physical abuse if there are any.

Keep in mind that this situation is sensitive, and the child may feel ashamed, embarrassed, anxious, scared, and distraught. A little compassion will go a long way.

It's important to talk about Good Touch and Bad Touch, so your child knows the difference. Talk to them about sexual abuse and date rape when you feel the time is right. Teach your child about consent and respecting boundaries when the answer of No is given.

I'll leave it up to you to do your research and to figure out which approach is best for you. The important thing is that you let your child know that they can feel comfortable coming to you in situations like this. Reassure them that you will believe them.

Don't be afraid of losing friends or family members if they happen to be an abuser. No abuser is above the law; I don't care if they have millions of dollars and can afford the best team of lawyers, or if they are an outstanding member of the community.

Pay close attention to your child's behavior around family members. For example; if your child was comfortable around Uncle Frank or Aunt June and has displayed healthy behavior such as sitting on their laps, hugging and happy to see them and the child's behavior changes drastically; that is a red flag.

If that same child shows signs of fear, anxiety when they know Uncle Frank or Aunt June is coming over or they don't want to interact with them, something is wrong.

Talk to your child, ask questions but don't force your child to interact because you feel it's rude. Don't force your child to give hugs if it's clear they don't want to.

The safety of your child should come first. They are counting on you to protect them.

About the Author

Hannah is a new author with this being her first self-published book; she was able to complete the writing process in under three weeks. Hannah is a Jane of All Trades; with experience in the automotive industry, baking, cake decorating, and she has written content for various web pages. She holds certificates in Safe Food Handling, Phlebotomy, Bookkeeping, and First Aid. Hannah is also a proud ally for the LGBTQ community.

For those that wish to collaborate with the author or get in touch for business purposes, please send your request to hannah.reinbeck@outlook.com or you can follow Hannah Reinbeck on Facebook.

https://www.facebook.com/hannah.reinbeck.9

Follow Hannah on Twitter: https://twitter.com/HReinbeck

Follow Hannah's blog:
https://reinbeckstudio.wordpress.com/

Reviews can be left on Goodreads or on Amazon.

National Resources

RAINN, Rape Abuse Incest National Network
https://www.rainn.org/
800-656-4673 (800-656-HOPE)

Canadian Centre for Child Protection
https://www.protectchildren.ca/app/en/training

1 in 6, Online Support & Information For Men About
Sexual Abuse/Assault
https://1in6.org/

Cybertip!ca Canada's National Tip Line for Reporting
Online Sexual Exploitation of Children
https://www.cybertip.ca/app/en/report

Child USA
https://www.childusa.org/

Prevent Child Abuse America
http://preventchildabuse.org/

National Suicide Prevention Lifeline
https://suicidepreventionlifeline.org/
The Lifeline provides 24/7, free and confidential support for
people in distress.

Within the USA 1-800-273-8255 (1-800-273-TALK)
Within Canada 1-833-456-4566 or TEXT 45645
For Deaf/Hard of Hearing - 1-800-799-4889
For Spanish - 1-888-628-9454

Manufactured by Amazon.ca
Bolton, ON